Reflections on the Common W

C000219548

Feedi̇ ̇g ̇. God
God's Word ̇w.

SUSAN SAYERS

Kevin
Mayhew

D
733

First published in 2001 by KEVIN MAYHEW LTD
Buxhall, Stowmarket, Suffolk IP14 3BW
Email: info@kevinmayhewltd.com

These texts first appeared in *Living Stones – Complete
Resource Book, Year A*

9 8 7 6 5 4 3 2 1 0

ISBN 1 84003 787 3
Catalogue No 1500452

Cover design by Jonathan Stroulger
Edited by Katherine Laidler
Typesetting by Richard Weaver

Printed and bound in Great Britain

Foreword

These reflections on the weekly readings are not new material – they come from the Complete Resource Book in the *Living Stones* programme, which follows the Common Worship Lectionary in the Anglican Church. Their publication in this separate book – here covering the readings for Year A – has been widely requested from various sources and for various reasons.

- Those who cannot get to church often, or who receive communion at home or in hospital, would like some help with reading the weekly Bible passages so they can be spiritually fed, and feel more part of the ongoing exploration of Scripture by the rest of the congregation.

- Discussion groups deciding to focus on the following week's readings express a need for the collected reflections in a separate book so that each group member can have a copy.

- Individuals wanting to prepare themselves for the worship Sunday by Sunday, or reflect on the previous week's readings, would like a book to help them. *Feeding on God's Word* serves this need.

- Those leading intercessions and reading the Bible passages during worship would value the reflections to help in their preparation.

- Those planning work with children and young people would like each team member to have a copy of the Scripture references and the reflection on those readings in order to feed them spiritually and better inform their prayer and preparation. Their own insights can then be incorporated in their ministry.

- Those with the talk or sermon to prepare would like their own copy of the Bible references and reflections to jump-start sermon preparation.

So, having heard all the requests, here is the book! I hope it will be useful to you all. These reflections don't pretend to be anything more than my own thinking as I read and pray the Scripture passages for each week. But I do believe that as more and more people in the church commit them-selves to praying for God's guiding, reading the Bible sections for each Sunday, and reflecting on them with the help of a book like this, together with a good commentary where necessary, the whole people of God will be fed – properly fed in a deep and wholesome way.

We are called to be bread-sharers as Christians, and that includes both word and sacrament. As we share the meal of Scripture week by week, as well as the meal of bread and wine, we will be nourished and strengthened for the daily work of love to which God invites us.

SUSAN SAYERS

Contents

First Sunday of Advent

Thought for the day
We are to wake up and make sure we stay ready
for the second coming.

Reflection on the readings
Isaiah 2:1-5; Psalm 122
Romans 13:11-14; Matthew 24:36-44

The Church begins its new year on Advent Sunday with the
alarm clock jerking us out of sleep. There isn't even a snooze
button. There is rather a sense of urgency as we listen to the
readings.

First we have the vision seen by Isaiah of the last days,
with the holy hill of Jerusalem a centre of pilgrimage for
people from every nation. It is a picture of two-way traffic;
the pilgrims streaming towards the city from all directions
in order to understand and know God better, and the
Word of God pouring out from Jerusalem in all directions
to teach, explain and transform lives.

From our position in time we can appreciate the typical
and extraordinary nature of such prophecy, since in Jesus
the Word of God has indeed been pouring out from
Jerusalem to the rest of the world, and to the rest of time
during this last age before the end of all. And it is to him
that the people come in every generation to have their
lives transformed.

The Isaiah passage ends with a summons and an invitation to walk in the light of the Lord, and Paul takes this up
in his letter to the Romans. The armour of light that will
protect us from evil is the life of love spelt out by Jesus both
in teaching and example. So, as we begin our preparation

for Christmas, we are reminded of Jesus' humility in coming to live among us and show us the Way, and also of the future, when he will return in glory as righteous judge.

In the Gospel we have Jesus' own teaching about the last days, and discover that one thing we can be certain of is that the second coming cannot be predicted. No last-minute revision will be possible, then, and the regular coursework format is a more helpful model. We have to live our lives in constant readiness so that we are not taken by surprise. This is partly so that we can be prepared for death or the second coming, and partly so that we can enjoy that quality of eternity which means God is constantly coming to us even while we live out our earthly lives. We need to be ready to receive him at every moment of every day.

Second Sunday of Advent

Thought for the day
Get the road ready for the Lord!

Reflection on the readings
Isaiah 11:1-10; Psalm 72:1-7, 18-19
Romans 15:4-13; Matthew 3:1-12

Before any real changes can take place in our spiritual development, we have to come to the point of recognising where we are and wanting it to be better. All addicts and their families are painfully aware of the necessity to acknowledge the addiction and find it unbearable, before there is any real hope of kicking the habit. It is at the point when a situation finally becomes intolerable that we are galvanised into taking action to change things.

Living in exile, the people of Israel became acutely aware of their nation's need for good leadership, justice, integrity and peace. In today's passage from Isaiah we sense their longing, as they look forward to God providing what they know they need. Typically, the prophecy was fulfilled in far greater measure, since the kingdom of justice, peace and love – the kingdom of God proclaimed by Jesus – is still growing throughout the entire world.

John the Baptist's message of repentance once again recovered the urgency for people sorting their lives out, since the coming of the Messiah was imminent and they wanted to put things right and be ready, much as we might rush round clearing up the house just before guests are due to arrive – especially those guests we want to impress, or those who we know will notice the clutter! Often the clearing will be something we know has needed doing for ages; the arrival of guests simply reminds us that it has to be done.

So what about all that spiritual clutter and grime which we know needs sorting? Today the Gospel helps to nudge us into urgent action, recognising that we don't want things to stay as they are, and the effort of changing whatever needs changing is well worth it. God comes and knocks at the door of our hearts all the time – not just at the end of the world.

Third Sunday of Advent

Thought for the day

Great expectations.
Jesus fulfils the great statements of prophecy.

Reflection on the readings

Isaiah 35:1-10
Psalm 146:5-10 or Canticle: Magnificat
James 5:7-10; Matthew 11:2-11

John the Baptist's task had been to prepare people for the coming of the Messiah, and that placed him, with all the prophets before him, in the age before the coming of the kingdom. We recall how John had urged people to sort out their lives, stressing the possibility of judgement as the all-seeing God came among his people in person, and it is easy to see how John's enthusiasm had polished his hopes into a specific shape. This is something we are all prone to do.

While it helped the urgency and focus of John's message, the side effect was that when Jesus' ministry started to look different from his expectation John began to wonder if he'd been mistaken. The frustration and suffering of his imprisonment must have added to the undermining negatives.

What Jesus does is hold up the Isaiah prophecy as a checklist. If these signs of the kingdom are indeed happening, then John can trust that the promised Saviour is indeed at work, even if the style of his ministry is different from what he had imagined. It's all to do with our expectations. If we get into the way of fleshing these out completely through our imagination, we may find that we don't recognise the real thing when we see it.

So it is as well to stay flexible, holding on to what we do know for certain and keeping our minds open about the details. This is true for us when we try to imagine God, heaven, or the end of all things. They may look like the paintings and frescoes of the Old Masters, and they may not. We mustn't let our expectations become stunted or narrowed by a particular artist's impression. That is what happened when people expected the astronauts to see God above the clouds and were disappointed. Our great expectations of God will be fulfilled far in excess of anything we might imagine and entirely in keeping with his nature.

Fourth Sunday of Advent

Thought for the day

Through the willing participation of Mary and Joseph,
God is poised to come among his people as their Saviour.

Reflection on the readings

Isaiah 7:10-16; Psalm 80:1-7, 17-19
Romans 1:1-7; Matthew 1:18-25

Matthew, writing for a Hebrew audience, is keen to show
the Jewish people that Jesus is indeed the promised Messiah.
He draws attention to Isaiah's prophecy spoken to King
Ahaz, and sets out Jesus' credentials. Through Joseph, Jesus
is a descendant of King David; through Mary, this son, born
to a virgin, fulfils the ancient prophecy and turns out to be
'Immanuel' or 'God with us'.

It is not unusual for prophecies about short-term, immediate events to turn out to have resonances far in excess of
their original meaning. One familiar example is the call to St
Francis to 'repair my Church, which is in ruins'. It was far
more than one stone chapel which was eventually 'repaired';
the whole Church of God became refreshed and invigorated.

The expectant atmosphere of today's readings attunes
us to God's way of orchestrating events and working in
co-operation with his people. The stage is set, the timing is
right, and the focused light of all the hopes and longings
of generations is about to shine out in the person of Jesus.
Typically, we find God delighting in using the ordinari-
ness of good people so that extraordinary things can be
accomplished. Typically, he allows individual people to
know their own part in the action exactly as and when
they need to know it.

It is because Joseph is expecting God to be God that he is prepared to alter his sensible and considerate plan to make no loud accusations about Mary when divorcing her for assumed unfaithfulness. Whatever that dream was, it made him think again. Perhaps Mary had tried to tell him the truth and he hadn't been able to believe her before. We can only guess at how Mary felt before Joseph changed his mind.

God will still speak to us through our dreams, memories and feelings, if only we take the trouble to notice. They can often be our own personal parables, able to put us in touch with our true selves; enabling us to recognise God's ways forward which we haven't been able to see before.

Christmas Day

Thought for the day

The Word of God is made flesh. In the birth of Jesus
we see God expressed in human terms.

Reflection on the readings

Isaiah 52:7-10
Psalm 98
Hebrews 1:1-4 (5-12)
John 1:1-14

The well-loved reading from Isaiah resounds with hope. It
is not wishful thinking, talking about impossible dreams,
but rings with utter surety that God has revealed to his
attentive prophet, so that the good news can be shared
with all the people of Israel. There is a great sense of
excitement, like the stirring in a great crowd as word gets
round that the famous and adored person they have been
waiting for is about to arrive. Today God has arrived in
person to live with the people of his creation, sharing their
humanity in order to save them.

The writer of Hebrews chooses this to introduce his
whole teaching: in the past God had spoken through his
prophets, but from the Incarnation onwards we are looking at an entirely new and dynamic experience, as God
speaks to us in person, through Jesus, the Son of God.

The introduction to John's Gospel helps us to see the
extraordinary depth of the meaning of God's 'Word', fling-
ing us back to the emerging creation from chaos, and forward to the streams of people through the generations
who choose to receive the light of God's life to transform
them and the world they inhabit. Stretched out across it all

is the person of Jesus, expressing God's creative and redeeming love in a way we, as humans, can understand. No darkness can ever extinguish the hope of this light.

First Sunday of Christmas

Reflection on the readings

Isaiah 63:7-9; Psalm 148
Hebrews 2:10-18; Matthew 2:13-23

One of the truths recognised in our readings today is that
the work of redemption cannot be done at arm's length. No
rescue operation can be carried out successfully without
someone being prepared to brave the dangers and go in to
share the conditions of those who need rescuing; only by
being this close can the rescuer bring the trapped to freedom. As the Isaiah passage acknowledges, 'It was no mes-
senger or angel but his presence that saved them', and in
the person of Jesus, being born into the human condition to
live a human life with human temptations and dangers,
this presence became a practical reality.

There is a wonderful sense in Psalm 148 of the entire created world welcoming God's creative Word, and the passage
from Hebrews emphasises the special link Jesus has with the
rest of us. We share flesh and blood with the incarnate One –
God made human. And the side effects of that involvement
are itemised clearly in the events following Jesus' birth, as
told by Matthew. Although the Christmas cards usually
show an idyllic scene of peace and joy, the real and dangerous world we all know is just outside the stable door.

In today's Gospel we find that Jesus has been born into
our familiar world of ruthless ambition, cruelty and

despair, of rejection and wandering, of isolation and fear. It reminds us that our God does not hold himself remote from our sufferings but is part of them, prepared to share with us the vulnerability of a baby refugee, bundled up in the night and taken off to a strange country in a life and death situation. It is God's willingness to be utterly immanent that means we really can trust him through the searing pain of life as well as its light and comfortable times.

Joseph gives us an inspiring example of committed attentiveness to God's leading, so that God can use his gifts of practical and efficient organisation to keep this child and his mother safe.

Second Sunday of Christmas

Thought for the day

The grace and truth revealed in Jesus show God's
freely-given love; through Jesus, God pours out his
blessings on us and gives us real freedom.

Reflection on the readings

Ecclesiasticus* 24:1-12 (* also called Sirach)
Canticle: Wisdom of Solomon 10:15-21
Ephesians 1:3-14; John 1:(1-9) 10-18

It is an amazing thought that there was never a time for
God when he was not yearning for all his creation to be
brought into a close, loving relationship as family members.
There is the breathtaking cosmic breadth of such a harmony, and at the same time the intimate, personal invitation
to each person throughout all time and space. Even as our
world was forming, God was longing for you and me and
our loved ones to be his own sons and daughters, enjoying
his love and responding to it.

The moment of Incarnation, which we celebrate at
Christmas, marks a new stage in the journey towards the
fulfilment of that longing and outreach. As Jesus, in the
ordinary, messy process of childbirth, emerges into the
world of human existence, the possibility is there for our
salvation. The Law, given through Moses, was of great
value, but with Jesus we have what the Law could never
give – God's freely-given grace in a totally loving human
life, to sort out our sin once and for all.

Mary and Joseph were happy to receive this child into
their home and their lives, and the receiving was very costly.
There have always been many who consider that receiving

Jesus Christ into their lives is too costly and they are not pre-pared to make that commitment. It is right that we sit down and count the cost before committing ourselves, and it is true that receiving Jesus is likely to be disruptive and is, in worldly terms, complete foolishness.

Paradoxically, receiving Jesus is also the way to such blessings and freedom of spirit that those who have taken the plunge would not have anything any different. Living in that close relationship with the God who is Father, Son and Spirit, allows us into a completely new dimension of living; quite apart from all the many blessings and joys, there is the underlying sense of it being profoundly good and right and true, and the place we were created to live in.

The Epiphany

Thought for the day

Jesus, the hope of the nations, is shown to the world.

Reflection on the readings

Isaiah 60:1-6; Psalm 72:(1-9) 10-15
Ephesians 3:1-12; Matthew 2:1-12

Beginning with one person (Abraham) and developing to embrace one family and eventually one nation, God has painstakingly planted the seed of salvation and nurtured it until the whole earth is involved. Isaiah had sensed that day in terms of a sunrise dawning with the light of day on a world of darkness, with all the hope and joy and relief that a new day can bring after a long, dark night. Probably this was one of the prophecies these magi had read as they studied the signs of the sky and wondered about life's meaning. And perhaps it was then that they felt stirring in them a profound calling to be, in person, those visitors who could symbolise the light dawning on the wider world. Certainly they must have been inspired by a powerful sense of urgency and necessity to make such a journey. And as they travelled, both physically and spiritually, towards Bethlehem, bearing the gifts laid down in those ancient scriptures, perhaps they were drawn by much more than a star. Jesus later proclaimed that anyone who sets out to search always finds.

Paul also knows himself to be commissioned to explain God's nature to the Gentiles. He is overwhelmed by the extraordinary way that the Christ has enabled us to approach the great and awesome God with freedom and confidence – as one of the family. And for all of us who are

Gentiles, the feast of the Epiphany is particularly one to celebrate, since it marks the truth that we too are part of God's salvation and can share the light of dawn.

The Baptism of Christ
First Sunday of Epiphany

Thought for the day

As Jesus is baptised, the Spirit of God rests visibly on him,
marking him out as the One who will save his people.

Reflection on the readings

Isaiah 42:1-9; Psalm 29
Acts 10:34-43; Matthew 3:13-17

In this season of Epiphany it is as if the mystery of the Incarnation is gradually being unfolded like a richly patterned carpet. Not that it will ever become totally understood this side of death, but even so, as year by year we examine it and marvel at it, truths of God's working and God's nature will gradually become apparent, and enable us increasingly to understand ourselves and our world. The knowledge of God is the beginning of wisdom.

Gestalt psychology talks of the 'Aha!' moment when fragments of knowledge suddenly form a pattern of fresh understanding in our minds. Peter's experience at Joppa led him to a sudden, new level of realisation about God's purposes: it was all so much bigger and wider than he had understood before. God was not the privately owned treasure of a few, but the glory and hope of the whole of humanity, in all places and all ages.

It must have been a similar 'Aha!' experience for Matthew, when, with his spiritual eyes open, he suddenly linked the moment of Jesus' Baptism with the prophecy from Isaiah. Perhaps you can remember an experience which has been marked with significance for you particularly in the light of subsequent developments? For those who have lived through the subsequent events of Christ's ministry, his death and resurrection, the Baptism of Jesus marks the taking on of the role of that servant described in the book of Isaiah.

It is no mistake that the words of God, heard by Jesus as he comes up out of the water, closely echo the opening words of Isaiah 42. Anyone with a working knowledge of the Isaiah passage would immediately call to mind the rest of the passage, with its hope and its tenderness.

Second Sunday of Epiphany

Thought for the day

Jesus is recognised and pointed out by John
to be God's chosen one.

Reflection on the readings

Isaiah 49:1-7; Psalm 40:1-11
1 Corinthians 1:1-9; John 1:29-42

Today, as we continue to think of Christ being shown, or revealed, to the world, there is another of the 'servant' readings from Isaiah. Set apart before birth, the servant has been brought into being to gather up Israel and bring her back into a right relationship with God, not through a dynamically successful campaign which the world might recognise and expect, but actually through worldly foolishness – failure, suffering and rejection.

Not only that, but as the plan unfolds it spills out of its original boundaries to include the possibility of salvation for the entire world. Gradually the prophet is starting to understand the scale of God's intended action.

We pick up echoes of the Gospel pictures of Jesus in that reading from Isaiah: the pre-natal cherishing, the light for the world, the redeemer, the homage paid by kings and important people. They are echoes that the people of Israel would have noticed, and they reveal Jesus as the One who fulfils the Old Testament writings in a most remarkable way.

John wants to tell everyone about it. It says a lot about John that he was able to direct his own disciples to Jesus. Probably with hindsight, the Gospel writer has John describing Jesus as 'God's Passover Lamb', with all the significance of sacrifice and the way to freedom which that suggests. Though he had been preparing them for this, it could still have been a moment to indulge the human instinct to be possessive, critical and defensive, yet in John we rather sense excitement and great enthusiasm.

In John's Gospel the emphasis is not so much on Jesus going out to find his disciples as them going to find him, and bringing one another along. We are aware of the attraction of this itinerant teacher and holy man, with his remarkable gift of discernment and wisdom. Can this really be the promised and long-awaited Messiah? It will only be time spent in Jesus' company that will enable these followers to decide about the truth of Jesus' identity.

And, as Paul writes in his letter to the church in Corinth, the same is true for all those who seek Jesus, whatever time or place they live in. As we spend time in Jesus' company we will find that it shows, and then others, spending time with us, may recognise the truth that Christ is living in us.

Third Sunday of Epiphany

Thought for the day

The prophecies of Isaiah are fulfilled in a new and
lasting way in Jesus of Nazareth.

Reflection on the readings

Isaiah 9:1-4; Psalm 27:1, 4-9
1 Corinthians 1:10-18; Matthew 4:12-23

At the time when Isaiah of Jerusalem spoke of the great
light of hope appearing in the darkness, and the yoke of
oppression finally being shattered to bring people freedom, the people of Israel were threatened with a takeover
bid and exile by Assyria, if they did not sort their values
and reconcile themselves to their God. All their dreams as
a nation could be wiped away if they were taken captive,
under the yokes of their conquerors, away from their own
beloved land, their city and their temple. (And eventually,
through the Babylonians, this did happen.)

Any of us who have watched our hopes and dreams
crash in pieces around us will have some idea of how such
an experience takes us on a journey through questioning,
self-doubt, anger, guilt, reassessment and eventually, hope-
fully, into a new maturity born of acceptance, greater self-
knowledge, forgiveness and the value of encountering
human suffering.

In their collective experience, the people are given hope,
both in the short term (Jerusalem was indeed saved from
the Assyrian threat) and, as we now can see, in the long
term, since Jesus startlingly clearly fulfils the prophet's
words as he treads the ground of Galilee, preaching, teaching and healing. The liberation he proclaims is not tied to

one generation whose threatened oppression is averted, but, as Paul emphasises in his letter to the church in Corinth, it also applies to every person sensing the liberating power of God's forgiving love which can set them free to live life to the full.

Fourth Sunday of Epiphany

Thought for the day

Jesus shows us in action the loving provision
of the God who made us.

Reflection on the readings

1 Kings 17:8-16; Psalm 36:5-10
1 Corinthians 1:18-31; John 2:1-11

Elijah went to Zarephath at God's instruction. He was
used to listening to God prompting him, and was willing
to go along with what he sensed God was asking him to
do. The widow, too, shows remarkable hospitality and
obedience, recognising Elijah as a holy man and gener-
ously sharing her last meal with this stranger.

In a similar way, the servants at the wedding recognise that
Jesus is speaking with an unusual authority, so they go along
with his strange instructions and risk the embarrassment of
pouring water into the cup of the master of the banquet. In the
event their faith is rewarded, as is the widow's, and people's
ordinary needs are met with finest quality provision.

John uses the 'water to wine' story as a sign to teach us a
bit more about who Jesus really is. The point of the water
turning into wine is not a magic trick, but a clue to help us
see that in Jesus the invisible, creative God is made visible
in human form and behaviour. Here we can see God's sen-
sitive understanding of our needs and daily difficulties,
his delight in working co-operatively with us in the provision, and his courteous manner of leaving us the space
to choose for ourselves whether to work with him or not.
God never forces our hand, but always respects our God-
given capacity for free will.

Our calling as the Church – being members of the Body of Christ – is to carry on that work of showing the compassion and love of our God in the situations we live in, to the people we meet in our ordinary lives every day. We need no letters after our names in order to do this, and there are no lower or upper age brackets. We simply need to be filled with the inner life of Christ so that the work of 'epiphany', or 'revealing', can continue in every place and in every generation.

Proper 1

Thought for the day

We are commissioned to live so that we shine like lights
which direct others on to God, the source of Light.

Reflection on the readings

Isaiah 58:1-9a (9b-12); Psalm 112:1-9 (10)
1 Corinthians 2:1-12 (13-16); Matthew 5:13-20

Salt and light can both make a great difference. Apart from
its wonderful preserving and disinfecting qualities, a pinch
of salt brings out the full flavour of other ingredients; light
allows everyone in the room to see the shape and texture of
all kinds of different objects which were hidden by darkness. And we as Christians are called to be salt and light to
the world. We are called to live so that our way of living
brings out in other people their full flavour, or potential;
we are called to live in a way that helps people see where
they are going, in the room, or context, of eternity.

We have all met people whose attitude and behaviour
towards us makes us shrivel up inside, and others in whose
company we feel accepted and acceptable, and therefore
free to be our true selves. It is loving reverence for one
another that makes the difference, and the Gospels are full
of incidents where people noticed this in their encounters
with Jesus.

If we behave as the salt of the earth, we will be content
to make ourselves available so that others feel free to
become more truly themselves, and we shall recognise the
need to be there, but not to overwhelm! Too heavy a dose

of salt kills off the flavour. If we behave as the light of the world we shall once again be in the role of enablers: we are at the service of the world, quietly enabling it to see more clearly. And again, we recognise the need to provide illumination, but not to blind or dazzle. Dazzling performances of ostentatious 'religion', such as those we heard about in the Isaiah reading, are not at all what God has in mind for his people, either then or now. What God wants is for the people in our world to be so impressed with the light we shine around that they want to find out where we get it from. Our shining is to set others off on their way to discover God for themselves.

Of course, we can only behave as salt and light if we are the genuine article, and are prepared to work co-operatively with God. That is where it is so helpful to have our faith 'earthed' in practical living. As Christians we all need to have our feet on the ground; we need to be engaged in the messy, hard work of caring, challenging injustice and offering practical help and support. Only then will our praises mean something, and our worship glorify God.

Proper 2

Thought for the day

To live God's way is to choose the way of life.

Reflection on the readings

Deuteronomy 30:15-20 or Ecclesiasticus 15:15-20
Psalm 119:1-8
1 Corinthians 3:1-9; Matthew 5:21-37

Jesus always insisted that he had not come to abolish the Law but to fulfil it. One of the challenging ways he does this is to take the ten commandments and work through them, pointing out not just the letter but the spirit of the law. Today we have an excerpt from this teaching in the Gospel reading, and by the time Jesus has finished preaching it is clear that the way of love is a demanding commitment, involving one's whole attitude and outlook as well as one's actual behaviour. The ten commandments are a kind of shorthand for this; they are the broad brush-strokes or guidelines, but not the whole picture. The danger is that people can feel they have completely fulfilled the law when they have simply taken care about the 'brush-stroke' examples; they can feel virtuous about not committing murder, for example, while their attitude to others continues to be destructive and patronising. With the law of love, expounded by Jesus, these attitudes are also considered 'murderous'.

Life is full of choices. Many times each day we have to decide whether to choose the way of life or the way of death, and unless we have taken time to decide what main

34

direction we want to walk in, we can become hopelessly confused. That is why it is good to use today and the reading from the Old Testament as a challenge: what direction do we really want to face?

If we make such a decision calmly and in our right mind, rather than waiting until we are in the grip of some temptation, then we are far more likely to have the courage to stand up for what we know in our hearts to be right.

As the community of Christ, we all need to be facing the 'Godwards' direction of life, using godly love as the compass. Then all the greater and lesser decisions to be made in our individual lives, and in our society and in the Church itself, can be worked out in line with these principles. Recognised mistakes are far healthier and easier to put right than unrecognised hypocrisy.

Proper 3

Thought for the day

We are called to be holy; to be perfect in our generous loving, because that is what God our Father is like.

Reflection on the readings

Leviticus 19:1-2, 9-18; Psalm 119:33-40
1 Corinthians 3:10-11, 16-23; Matthew 5:38-48

When those who were adopted as young children meet up with their birth parents, it is often startling and amusing to find that they share some mannerism which must have been inherited but had seemed more like a personal habit. When Jesus talks about our calling to be perfect in such things as generous loving, he gives as his reason the fact that God our Father is perfect. We, as God's children, need to share his characteristics – his 'mannerisms' – an example of which is a tendency to generosity of spirit which is lavish to the point of extravagance.

We are to be like 'chips off the old block', so that the way we live and behave demonstrates to everyone our spiritual parentage. This is not so much learned behaviour, in the way that one might act out a part in a drama production, but more like the natural result of being God's children. When we wake up each morning allowing that to happen, and giving the living God access to our minds, emotions and bodies, then God's natural characteristic of generous loving will start to show through without our having to contort ourselves to achieve it.

Jesus is trying to get us to examine not only our actions but also our motives and our attitudes. We are to think at all times not 'What can I gain out of this?' but 'What can I give away and how can I serve here?' The worldly perception of perfection is measured by a completely different set of success criteria. The ever-present danger is that even Christians soak up the worldly values of success and start applying them to spiritual matters. That leads into the legalistic and judgemental zones which Jesus so deplored. God's way is as happy to use our failures as our strengths, our muddles and mistakes as much as our slick, poised control.

God's way has us viewing cancelled trains and traffic jams, undeserved criticism and demanding phone calls as unscheduled opportunities for learning and possibly serving. It is our God-filled attitude to them that unclenches the tight jaw and relaxes the facial muscles! It may also be what enables us to express our concerns calmly and sort out a workable alternative without being churned up inside with resentment and hidden rage. God's way of generous loving is not only the best way to live; it is also the way God designed us to be, and the way in which we are most fulfilled and most effective.

Second Sunday before Lent

Thought for the day

God is creative and good; seeking his rule, as our priority, will mean that everything else falls into place.

Reflection on the readings

Genesis 1:1-2:3; Psalm 136 or 136:1-9, 23-26
Romans 8:18-25; Matthew 6:25-34

As soon as we become aware of the fact that we are individuals, living in somewhere called 'place', the natural human reaction is to start wondering about it. Why are we here? Who are we? How are we here? These are universal, important questions, and enable us to become fully ourselves.

This later version of the creation of the world in Genesis 1 is a glorious poem exploring the deep human wondering, and recognising that in some way God is at the very centre and source of it all, calling creation into being through the creative power of his love. In some sense the parental longing for children and the creative urge of the artistic are the human reflection of the divine love which fashioned us.

Today's readings celebrate the overarching and undergirding love and care of our God. Jesus shows a wonderfully childlike and relaxed assurance about this, which he longs for us to know and share. So much of our time is spent anxiously worrying about things over which we have no control, and it is not God's will that we should go through life harassed and agitated like this. We can learn much from young children here. Toddlers are so good at accepting the way they drop off to sleep in one place and wake up somewhere completely different, while we in the meantime have vacuumed and washed up, fixed them into the car seats, driven through the roadworks and emerged at the supermarket. The sleeping child trusts that the parent will be looking after them. Humans take time to learn to distrust.

Jesus is recommending that we relearn that trust in our Parent God as soon as possible, so we can live freely, basking in the faithful love that will never let us down. It is this security which enables us to meet and cope with all the inevitable stresses and strains of living, because our roots are firmly fixed in what is greater and more profound than anything else.

If that is in place, the rest becomes manageable and less threatening. And once we are feeling our survival unthreatened, we are able and willing to take risks, and accept disappointments and pain without being overwhelmed by them. Eventually, as Paul suggests, all things will be accomplished and transformed.

Sunday before Lent

Thought for the day

In Jesus the full glory of God is revealed and encountered.

Reflection on the readings

Exodus 24:12-18; Psalm 2 or Psalm 99
2 Peter 1:16-21; Matthew 17:1-9

Today's Old Testament reading is full of the mystery and awe of God's majesty, symbolised by the devouring fire at the top of the holy mountain of Sinai, and the cloud into which only Moses, the one set apart by God, is allowed to enter. All the people are left down at the bottom of the mountain, gazing up at its distant holiness and the spectacle of almighty God's transcendent power. Chapter 25 goes on to relate the commission God gave Moses on this occasion, to make preparations for building a special sanctuary – a tabernacle – where God will dwell among his people in what became known as the Ark of the Covenant.

The Gospel takes us to another mountain made holy by God's presence there. Matthew tells us that Jesus has taken three of his disciples with him, and as he is praying, communicating directly with his Father, he becomes transfigured, so that Peter, James and John witness the glory of God shining in the human body of Jesus. And into that intimate conversation walk Moses and Elijah, representing the Law and the prophets. To the disciples and to Matthew's original readers, well acquainted with the scriptures, the echoes of Moses' experience on Mount Sinai will have been obvious. It must have seemed almost like a time warp, and perhaps, in a sense, it is, since at such moments of eternity we are as much present with

Moses in the holy cloud and Elijah listening to the still small voice as we are with God speaking through Jesus and drawing together past and future at a moment of intense reality and depth of love.

No wonder, then, that Simon Peter refers to the subsequent conversation of God and Moses, and wants to build tabernacles so that God's transcendence can become immanent among his people. But Peter has not yet grasped the extraordinary extent of God's immanence which has now gone far beyond tabernacles. In the person of Jesus, as the transfigured glory shows, God is now personally and intimately among his people in a way never possible before, and the approaching act of self-giving love on the cross, and triumph over death, are going to mean that the personal closeness will be possible far and wide in all places and in all generations, including ours. It is vital that these followers of Jesus understand something of this, and there is urgency in God's voice heard by them encouraging them to trust the amazing identity of his Son and to hang on his words. They have been shown God's glory on the top of the mountain so that they will be better able to recognise God's immanence at the bottom, when the cloud has faded.

First Sunday of Lent

Thought for the day
Jesus knows all about temptation;
and he can deal with our sin.

Reflection on the readings
Genesis 2:15-17; 3:1-7; Psalm 32
Romans 5:12-19; Matthew 4:1-11

Temptation always has that element of good sense which makes the sin seem appealing and plausible. We can imagine that Eve could be praised for wanting to stretch the limits of her and Adam's potential; wisdom for the human race was arguably a sensible step in promotion terms. The darker side of temptation is that the illusory good sense masks the basic clear fact that doing or saying or thinking this particular thing is simply wrong. In Adam and Eve's case the serpent's suggestion went against God's instructions, and resulted in them choosing to be disobedient. Typically, what initially looks so attractive turns out to cause misery and confusion. The pattern of temptation and sin is a depressing one, and one for which we can all bring regretful and painful examples to mind.

At which point, God's plan for mending and healing springs thankfully into action in the person of Jesus, who is tempted in exactly the same way we are. First, Satan goes for personal well-being and comfort: making stones into bread. When Jesus stands firm on what is really important, rather than self-centred needs, Satan goes for another favourite: self-doubt. He suggests a good and foolproof way for Jesus to test whether or not he really is God's Son. But, if we look at Jesus' answer, we find he is remembering that putting God to the test like this, as the people of Israel had done at Massah in the wilderness, is an insult to God's love and faithfulness.

So Satan, homing in on Jesus' loyalty to his Father and his respect and love for him, suggests a clever and speedy way to please God by claiming all the people and presenting them to the Father, just as he is genuinely hoping to do. There's a big catch here, though. Jesus will need to pay for the privilege by worshipping Satan. Satan has overstepped the mark here, and made it plain who he is, and how evil the plan is, so the battle is over, at least for the moment.

If we can copy Jesus in clinging on to the real underlying truths during our temptations, they will eventually emerge to be seen as obviously wrong. The danger in temptation is the point when we are being won over by the persuasive attraction and plausibility, so that our hold on what is right and good is temporarily loosened. It is as if we are temporarily 'off balance' and therefore easy to knock down.

Thankfully, Jesus did much more than wade through terrible temptation without sinning. He went on to take on freely the punishing cursed death which results from sin, and so opened the way back into the garden of hope and promise. As we hold on to Jesus in faith, he enables us to exchange lasting death for full and everlasting life.

Second Sunday of Lent

Thought for the day

Anyone who believes in Jesus can know his power
to save and set us free.

Reflection on the readings

Genesis 12:1-4a; Psalm 121
Romans 4:1-5, 13-17; John 3:1-17

If you want to join the local fitness centre or golf club, it's
quite clear what you do – you pay your membership sub-
scription and agree to abide by the rules so that you can
enjoy the privileges. Anyone expecting to enjoy the privileges without being fully paid-up members would be
shown the door. This is rather how the Jewish people in
the early church community felt about the new Gentile
believers. They felt they ought to become full members of
the Jewish religion in order to take advantage of Jesus'
saving work.

Paul is anxious to point out that the real heritage is not
through genetics or traditional customs like circumcision.
It comes instead through faith. Abraham received God's
promise that he would become the father of many nations
when he took God at his word and uprooted his whole
life. Anyone who has that kind of faith in God is, in effect,
a descendant of Abraham.

Nicodemus was struggling with God's broad-mindedness
as shown in the way Jesus is living, welcoming the margin-
alised and the sinners. Can he really be the Messiah? When
he came to talk things over with Jesus one night Jesus
explained to him that understanding God's ways requires
being born into a new dimension. The pragmatic Nicodemus

is still puzzled as he is used to taking everything literally and knows people can't scrunch up into womb shapes when they are grown up. But Jesus is trying to help him think spiritually, rather than literally. He tells him that living by faith in God – living 'in the Spirit' – is rather like being blown along in a strong wind, and it's no good trying to cling on to stationary objects to anchor ourselves or we won't be able to allow ourselves to be moved along in God's direction and at God's speed.

That is very difficult because we all tend to want to retain our independent control in life, and allow God access to some areas but not to others. We can thank Nicodemus for being honest about his narrowness and preconceived ideas, thereby giving us the courage to talk over with Jesus the things which puzzle and disturb us about our faith. This is far more healthy and far more likely to promote eventual spiritual growth than denying such feelings to ourselves or feeling guilty about them. Questions are a tried and tested route to understanding, and do in themselves require of us a certain trust, because through our questions we are moving out into uncharted territory.

We can be reassured that wherever God leads us, however strange or disturbing the journey, however our assumptions are challenged, moving in God is an ultimately safe and good place to be, and we will be fully alive both in this age and in eternity.

Third Sunday of Lent

Thought for the day

God both knows us completely and loves us completely;
meeting us where we are, he provides us with living
water, to satisfy all our needs.

Reflection on the readings

Exodus 17:1-7; Psalm 95
Romans 5:1-11; John 4:5-42

Whether it's a blind date, a job interview or meeting the
future in-laws for the first time, we are likely to take extra
care with how we look and behave, wanting to show our
best selves in order to give a good impression. That is a
kind of game we all play. If we really thought about it we'd
realise that it has to do with not trusting these strangers to
notice our good qualities unless we underline them a bit
with some visuals. We may suspect that if they really knew
our ordinary messy selves, before they had got to know
and enjoy us better, they may well disapprove or dislike us.

With God it's different. We can't 'dress to impress'
because God knows us inside out already. When Jesus had
that conversation with the woman at Jacob's well in
Samaria she was stunned by the sudden realisation that
Jesus knew her; he understood where she was coming
from and what was important to her, where she was weak
and where she was strong. He understood her potential as
well as her mistakes. So it did not feel like invaded privacy
because, along with the full knowledge, she sensed full
acceptance.

Perhaps you have felt yourself shrivel up in the company of those who seem to judge and condemn, and open

out and blossom in the company of those who love and delight in you. In the level, direct gaze of the loving God we can all be reassured that we are both known and accepted. That accepting love is like living water which our spirits need to survive and thrive and grow.

Out in the wilderness the people of Israel were well aware of their needs, but they were looking backwards nostalgically, rather than trustingly at the living God to supply them. And that too is a very human reaction. We tend to try all kinds of inferior, stagnant or temporary water supplies rather than going directly to the source of living water which never runs dry, is guaranteed pure and wholesome for us, and is exactly what we need at every changing moment of our journey through life.

Fourth Sunday of Lent
Mothering Sunday

Thought for the day

Thanking God for our earthly opportunities for mothering and being mothered, we also remember the mothering parenthood of God.

Reflection on the readings

Exodus 2:1-10 or 1 Samuel 1:20-28
Psalm 34:11-20 or Psalm 127:1-4
2 Corinthians 1:3-7 or Colossians 3:12-17
Luke 2:33-35 or John 19:25-27

Both Moses and Samuel have touching mother-and-baby stories related in the Old Testament. Samuel was the result of Hannah's answered prayer; she did not forget this once the better times came but kept faith with God, which meant that the whole people of Israel benefited from a spiritual leader and adviser of remarkable integrity and wisdom. Moses inherited the resourcefulness and perseverance in the face of threats shown by his mother as she hid her son among the bulrushes where Pharaoh's daughter was bound to be enchanted by the baby's vulnerability and disarming innocence.

And then we have the words of Simeon, spoken to Mary, when, as a young mother, she and Joseph take the baby Jesus into the temple. Or we stand with the heartbroken Mary at the foot of the cross where her promising son hangs dying a cursed death inflicted by the army of occupation and demanded by the religious leaders and teachers.

In all these mothering stories there is no attempt to sugar or sentimentalise what mothering involves – the pain and aching, the bewildered confusion and times of misunderstanding and grief, as well as all the joy and affection, shared laughter and the delight in watching a human being develop and mature. The Bible tells about the real human condition, and in all this mothering and being mothered we sense something of God's mothering, or parenting, of us. When on the cross Jesus commits his grieving mother into the care of the disciple he loves, we are seeing a wonderful example of the way we are all given to one another to care for and look after.

That is a two-way process: we need to cultivate the art of receiving the mothering as well as giving it. We need to recognise that it may well involve both times of great joy and deep sorrow as we increasingly bear one another's burdens and suffering, and watch one another developing spiritually. Mothering of this sort is rooted in God's parenting of us, and will break our hearts of stone and give us tender hearts of flesh that are willing to give one another both support and space.

Fifth Sunday of Lent

Jesus is the resurrection and the life. He can transform
death and despair, in any form, into life and hope.

Reflection on the readings
Ezekiel 37:1-14; Psalm 130
Romans 8:6-11; John 11:1-45

Things don't come much deader than dry scattered bones.
It is a powerful image of the totally hopeless, without even
a whispered memory of life. Ezekiel the prophet speaks
God's unlikely hope to a dislocated and despairing people.
In the hands of God there is no abandonment but promise
of restoration, bone by bone, sinew by sinew, inbreathed by
the Creator's breath.

Psalm 130 echoes the dazed amazement at the way God
proves again and again that with the Lord there is mercy
and fullness of redemption. In Romans we find the same
realisation worked out in a more cerebral way, celebrating
the profound truth, born of real experience, that Spirit-filled
life is a completely new and fulfilling life, in comparison
with which other life seems like a kind of deadness.

And in today's Gospel reading we hear the whole narra-
tive of Lazarus and his sisters, living through his dying
and death, while the Lord of life is elsewhere. It is an
evocative story, with Jesus portrayed at his most human,
and many layers of meaning packed into the event. Why
did Jesus delay? What about those conversations, first
with Martha and then with Mary?

John is wanting to tell us deep truths about Jesus' total
humanity and divinity; if ever a story revealed the nature

of Emmanuel – 'God-with-us' – then this is it. The practical, less emotional Martha is better able to grasp the logic of what it means for the Lord of life to be present, whereas Mary is simply devastated and feels wounded by Jesus' absence which doesn't make sense to her.

We may recognise this terrible sense of loss and distance when in our own lives we feel God ought to be there yet he seems not to be; and Jesus himself knew it on the cross: 'My God, why have you forsaken me?' But it is this raw grief in all its honesty and candour which tears Jesus' heart and shakes him with agonised weeping. With us, too, he is there at such times of raw pain, sharing our searing pain and grief and weeping with us.

Jesus, as the Lord of life, is God's voice speaking right into the darkness of death and drawing out life.

Palm Sunday

Thought for the day

Jesus rides into Jerusalem cheered by the crowds.
Days later crowds will be clamouring for his death.

Reflection on the readings

Liturgy of the Palms:
Matthew 21:1-11; Psalm 118:1-2, 19-29
Liturgy of the Passion:
Isaiah 50:4-9a; Psalm 31:9-16; Philippians 2:5-11
Matthew 26:14-27:66 or Matthew 27:11-54

Today we begin the heightened drama of the walk through
a week known as holy. Since Christmas we have traced the
life of Jesus through his birth, childhood, Baptism and
preparation in the wilderness, and touched on the main
areas of his ministry; and now we come to that final week
of his earthly life. All the Gospel writers move into notice-
ably greater detail in their narratives, with these events taking up a sizeable proportion of each Gospel. The words
and events are carefully and thoroughly recorded, in keeping with the intense significance of these days which focus
all of life before them and all that has happened since.

Quite deliberately, the readings and liturgy take us on a
roller-coaster of spiritual experience. We stand with the
ecstatic crowds waving palm branches and celebrating the
entry into Jerusalem, the holy city, by Jesus the Messiah.
There is great hope and expectation that final things are
drawing to accomplishment. We are poignantly aware that
Jesus is both acknowledging the crowd's excitement at his
kingship and also trying to show them something of the

true nature of his kingship which has nothing to do with temporal power and wealth or narrow nationalism.

And then we are gripped by the detailed seriousness of all that led up to the crucifixion, like a profound family memory indelibly written on hearts and handed down with great care and reverence from generation to generation. We both cry out against what is happening and also know it to be necessary and inevitable. We both balk at the way people could treat Jesus, the Lord of life, and also know that we do it ourselves every day. We recognise the utter failure and futility of it all and also know it to be the strangest and most complete victory for the entire world.

Easter Day

It is true. Jesus is alive for all time. The Lord of life cannot be held by death. God's victory over sin and death means that new life for us is a reality.

Reflection on the readings

Acts 10:34-43 or Jeremiah 31:1-6; Psalm 118:1-2, 14-24
Colossians 3:1-4 or Acts 10:34-43
John 20:1-18 or Matthew 28:1-10

Just as in the story of creation, God rests on the Sabbath, when his great, creative work is complete, so now there has been a Sabbath of rest following the completion of this great re-creative work of salvation. In Jesus' last cry on the cross, 'It is finished!', there was the sense of accomplishment and completion, and now, in the dark of early morning on Sunday, the tomb is no place to stay and linger.

It is wonderfully human that all the accounts of the resurrection are slightly different; just as in any life-changing, dynamic event, people's accounts of the details are fused with their attempts to interpret and grasp the significance of what has happened. What is clear beyond all doubt is that somehow they began to understand the extraordinary truth – that Jesus had died but was no longer dead, in the human sense of the word. He was totally alive, but not in the merely human way – like Lazarus, for instance – where it would only be a matter of time before death came again.

Jesus, having gone into death with the power of life, and with his selfless love untarnished, could not be held there, but broke out into a new kind of life which is never going to end. Compared with this life, death is shadowy and powerless; it is temporary suffering and a journey of darkness which leads into unending daylight.

Peter and the other disciples can tell it from first-hand experience. They have actually seen Jesus fully alive, and have even eaten and drunk with him. Not that they were any different from the rest of us in finding it all impossible at first to imagine and believe; Jesus had been preparing them for this, but they still didn't really expect it to happen. After all, full life like this, after that very definite and horrific death through crucifixion, is simply impossible. Isn't it?

Like a catapult that has been pulled and stretched right back in one direction, the force of a sudden change of direction is very vigorous. Having been through the bewildered acceptance of Jesus' death and having lived a couple of days with numbing absence, the truth shoots them into a passion for telling everyone the amazing news, once they are equipped with the Holy Spirit's anointing. It is those who are witnesses to what God has done in their lives who tell the good news of the Gospel for real. And that is what convinces others of a truth which has the power to transform their entire life, both in time and after death.

Second Sunday of Easter

Thought for the day

Through the risen Jesus we have a living hope
which will never spoil or fade.

Reflection on the readings

Acts 2:14a, 22-32; Psalm 16
1 Peter 1:3-9; John 20:19-31

In these Easter readings we have a rather intriguing perspective, since we hear first from the post-Holy Spirit days and then go back to the events close to the Resurrection in the Gospel reading. It has the effect of sharpening our senses, making us more aware of the changes in this group of disciples. Peter is confident and speaks out in authority to the listening crowd. He seems to have got his act together, and has obviously been reflecting deeply on the way in which Jesus has fulfilled the prophecies of Scripture in a quite extraordinary and largely unexpected way. He has been able to see how his Jewish heritage is wonderfully enriched and given fresh meaning, and he cannot wait to share these insights with his fellow Israelites, so that they, too, can experience the liberation of living the new life.

His enthusiasm and confidence continue in the reading from 1 Peter, where he encourages those having to endure very real and terrifying suffering for their faith. Only someone who had also suffered would be able to make such assertions with any credibility, and Peter speaks from the heart. He knows what it feels like to be scared of standing up for what you believe in; he knows what it feels like to fail miserably after good intentions, when you try to do things in your own strength. And he also knows that even the most timid of us can cope with anything when we are living the risen life in the power of Jesus Christ.

The Gospel shoots us back to a very anxious group of people, terrified of the Jewish authorities even though they are (apart from Thomas at this stage) actually convinced that Jesus is alive. Although they know he is risen, they have not yet accessed the power of that risen life, and have at present the boldness of mashed potato.

What Jesus does is to reassure them by his visible and tangible presence. There is a wonderful sense of normality in his greeting. When someone we love has died, and our life seems thrown up in the air and is falling slowly in pieces around us, what we crave is for things to be back to normal again. Jesus understands this, and provides his friends with the reassuring presence they need. Then he breathes into them, as Adam was breathed into at the creation. This breath is what gives the disciples the power of new life, and with it comes the conferring of authority, whose hidden side is responsibility. Like Jesus they are sent out, as the word 'apostle' proclaims, to tell the good news with confidence in the living spirit of Jesus.

Thomas was also scared. He was scared, like many of us, of being taken for a ride – of belief being only wish-fulfilment. Thomas was going to stick to an honest recognition of where he stood until he had definite proof. When he is offered it, he finds he no longer needs it; the sight of Jesus is quite enough. Suddenly prophetic, Jesus acknowledges the faith of all those, including us, who do not have the benefit of visual and tactile sightings of Jesus, and yet are still able to believe in him and share his risen life.

Third Sunday of Easter

Thought for the day

Jesus explains the scriptures
and is recognised in the breaking of bread.

Reflection on the readings

Acts 2:14a, 36-41; Psalm 116:1-4, 12-19
1 Peter 1:17-23; Luke 24:13-35

Once again our first reading takes us into the middle of a crowd of people who are listening, devastated, to Peter, as he speaks powerfully about who Jesus is, and the terrible truth begins to dawn on them that they have all been instrumental in annihilating the Messiah, the hope of the nations. Yet Peter is not proclaiming God's imminent judgement but his fulsome mercy and offer of forgiveness. Somehow this God of limitless love is able to take anything and transform it; we can know this for certain because in Jesus he has taken death itself – and a cursed death – and turned it into Resurrection, with new and lasting life.

The Psalm for today celebrates that wonderful sense of release as God frees us from our chains, whatever they are; and in his letter, Peter writes of the cost of our freeing, which points to such an extraordinary love that it draws out love in us both towards God and towards one another.

We are then taken back to that period of numb misery after the crucifixion, when all hope seemed dead for ever. We are on a road, with two grieving and confused disciples of Jesus, walking away from Jerusalem towards the town of Emmaus where they lived. Why was it that Jesus drew alongside these particular people, we may wonder. Perhaps his heart went out to them as a shepherd might look at his sheep who are in pain and lost and don't understand. Certainly Cleophas, who presumably shared this detailed account with Luke, recognises the low point their faith had reached and doesn't try to hide that.

Jesus walks along in the same direction they are going, leading them patiently and carefully to see the hints and clues in the scriptures which point to the necessity for the Messiah to suffer and die before being glorified. When they near their home, Jesus gives them the option of taking his words thus far and no further. He never forces his company on us. But the disciples can't bear to part from him now, and as he breaks bread they suddenly realise who he is, at which moment he no longer needs to be visible to them. They rush straight back, seven or eight miles, to Jerusalem, in their utter joy and excitement.

With us, too, Jesus draws alongside and helps us understand the words of scripture. He gives us the option of walking with him no further. And whenever we invite him to stay, he comes in and shares bread with us. Whenever we meet together and break bread in Jesus' name, Jesus is there in person among us, and very often that presence is almost tangible as we sense his love and his peace.

Fourth Sunday of Easter

Thought for the day
Jesus, the Good Shepherd, has come
so that we may have life in rich abundance.

Reflection on the readings
Acts 2:42-47; Psalm 23; 1 Peter 2:19-25; John 10:1-10

Reading today's passage from Acts 2 is rather like being given a photo album of the Early Church to look through. There are snapshots of the community which give us some idea, in a few sentences, of how it all worked and what made it hum. We see the people at worship, making their financial commitments and decisions, working in loving service wherever there are needs, and simply enjoying themselves together. We can imagine similar snapshots with the familiar faces of our own church communities. Permeating all the worship and all the action is a fresh amazement at the power of God; the Resurrection plugs the Church into the reality of God's dynamic immanence. In God's frame of reference, it is still only like yesterday that the Resurrection happened; every Sunday we can 're-member it' – in other words, 'put it all together again' in our minds so that we never lose the freshness.

This freshness will affect the way we live out our faith, as the passage from 1 Peter reminds us. It is so easy to get back into the old habits and mind-sets where we are entitled to moan and protest about any hardship or punitive treatment we don't consider we deserve. But Peter takes issue with that way of thinking. Suppose we turned it on its head, taking Christ as our example? Suppose we were able to consider all those unjustified sufferings not simply as painful (which they certainly are, of course) but also as a kind of privilege to be taken to God for transforming, rather like raw diamonds which we might take to be expertly cut and polished.

Could we then treat those insults and unkindnesses towards us with more grace and reverence – as raw hope in the making, perhaps? And as we wrestled to live out God's foolishness like this, could it be that we would actually be involved in a huge and vital strengthening of the whole body of Christ, worked out in each of our individual battles, whenever joyful self-giving triumphed over self, and unlimited loving over presumed rights?

The possibility sets alarm bells ringing in us, as we recognise the risk of exposure and vulnerability involved in such complete self-giving. Are we prepared to trust God that much? Isn't it all too much to expect?

Today's Gospel shows us a God who is not out to get us, to steal from us or put us down. He is not in the business of destructive behaviour; he is not wanting to wear us down with guilt or demand of us more than we can possibly give. Sadly the Church has sometimes given this impression, and sent the sheep racing away in understandable alarm. But the image Jesus chooses is of a shepherd whom the sheep sense they can trust, and who will only use his power to provide wisely and faithfully for those in his care. In that care they are free to come and go, living out their lives doing what sheep do without panic or confusion.

What does that mean for us? We too are like sheep in the way we tend to panic and scatter, the way we are so vulnerable to following wrong values, empty and unsatisfying lifestyles, and unprincipled and irresponsible leaders. We desperately need the Good Shepherd, but need so much coaxing before we realise it. I sometimes wonder if the angels of heaven are standing around like the spectators at sheepdog trials, willing those sheep to go where they need to and cheering when they finally get the message!

Yet in the keeping of the Good Shepherd we are set free to live out our lives more truly as ourselves than ever before.

Fifth Sunday of Easter

Thought for the day

Jesus is the Way, the Truth and the Life, through whom
we can come into the presence of God for ever.

Reflection on the readings

Acts 7:55-60; Psalm 31:1-5, 15-16
1 Peter 2:2-10; John 14:1-14

Rocks are solid things, which makes them very strong as
foundations but exceedingly painful and obstinate to kick.
They do not give. This makes the rocky image given to us by
Peter, himself nicknamed 'the rock', such a splendid one for
helping us visualise the utter faithfulness and solid assurance of Jesus. Being built up on such a foundation is an excit-
ing prospect for the household of faith. And the building
depends on those living stones in every generation which
continue to be added to the great living temple of worship
and praise. Like stones we are to be strong in our faith, a
faith that is not merely existing but fully and dynamically
alive. What a Church it can be, when it is firmly set on the
foundation of Christ and built through his power alone with
the offered lives and gifts and sufferings and struggles of
millions and millions of ordinary human beings!

We have a wonderful example of just one of those living
stones to inspire us today. As we watch the young man,
Stephen, standing gazing into heaven as stones of hatred,
misunderstanding, misplaced zeal and righteous indignation are hurled at him, we can see how his faith fixes him
securely, even as he is being put to death. His loving forgiveness of his enemies proclaims the reality of his faith –
it stands the worst testing and still holds.

How does he do it, we may ask? Perhaps we find ourselves feeling not so much inspired as dampened by people who seem to have such great faith when we are trying to muddle along and are woefully aware of how inadequately we witness to Christ most of the time. Perhaps we feel more in common with Philip, as he tries so hard to understand what Jesus is saying, but is thinking on a completely different plane, unable to put the signs and clues together and come up with a meaningful answer. It took the death and resurrection of Jesus for things to suddenly start making sense to the disciples, and that is still true for us today. Still it is the death and resurrection of Jesus which enables everything else to make sense.

In the light of Jesus' death and resurrection we can grasp that he really is the Way, the Truth and the Life. It is through believing in this Jesus, who gave up his life in total self-giving love for us, and lived out for us in human terms the loving nature of almighty God, that we too can die to sin and be brought into a new life relationship with God which is valid both in time and eternity. So the Way is not a code of behaviour but a relationship with a person. And that is as basic to our human experience and need as the child/parent bonding which is also present from birth, rather than the codes of behaviour which are only later acquired.

It is a living, personal relationship that Jesus offers and hopes for us to accept. The relationship will never end, but will continue getting deeper and more satisfying, and continue developing and strengthening us in our faith, throughout our entire life.

Sixth Sunday of Easter

Thought for the day
The Spirit of truth, given to us,
enables us to discern the living, risen Christ.

Reflection on the readings
Acts 17:22-31; Psalm 66:8-20
1 Peter 3:13-22; John 14:15-21

It wasn't just that the Greek people were hedging their bets by building an altar to the unknown god. It was also part of their spirituality that in all their deities they were seeking to get in touch with the unknowable – the ultimate reality – which defies human knowing. That hit a chord with Paul, because he could see how Jesus was not only fulfilling the Judaic law, but also all the other genuine human attempts to grasp the mysteries of God's truth. They were right; if it weren't for Jesus, the essence of ultimate reality would continue to be hidden from our sight and understanding.

What God chose to do through the Incarnation was to draw close to his beloved people in such a way that they could see what this mystery we call God was like, in human terms of reference. That had to include a demonstration of what love means even in the face of total cursing and rejection, and God went ahead and showed that, too, in the death of Jesus. It had to include a demonstration of how this power of creative life is even stronger than death – which is, in human terms, annihilation and destruction. So God went ahead and did it. It's called the Resurrection.

In our continued reading of Peter's letter, we are advised to hold on, literally for dear life, to this Christ, who is God's dependable love, and brings us through all suffering with the dynamism of resurrection life. Peter likens our Baptism into faith, using the dramatic symbol of drowning and washing, to the way Noah and his family were brought through the destructive flood waters to a new life experience and a fresh start. And we know we are in that new life by the experience of being alive in Christ.

The reading from John's Gospel unpacks that for us a bit. What do people look like who are living Christ's risen life? How would we know one if we saw one? John states Jesus' words with a straightforward bluntness that does not let us hide behind high-sounding and noble ideals: it is the way we live obediently to the commands of love that sets us apart and proves that we are followers of the way of Christ. Well-intentioned, but never getting round to it, is not part of the deal. Neither are excuses, cop-out clauses or allowable exceptions. It is quite clear from today's Gospel reading that if we really love, we will live that love out, not in a fair-weather friendship, but in a sacrificial way that often chafes and hurts, and leads us in ways we may not have taken by the comfort choice.

And what is the point of choosing such a path? What is in it for us? Jesus promises that, through the gift of the Spirit of Truth, we will become intimate friends with the almighty and merciful God, and will increasingly be honoured with discerning his presence, not as a memory or a hope, but as a real experience of the living person who brought us into being, redeemed us and loves us for ever.

Ascension Day

Thought for the day

Having bought back our freedom with the giving of his life, Jesus enters into the full glory to which he is entitled.

Reflection on the readings

Acts 1:1-11 or Daniel 7:9-14
Psalm 47 or Psalm 93
Ephesians 1:15-23 or Acts 1:1-11
Luke 24:44-53

The Ascension marks the end of Jesus' appearances on earth and his physical, historical ministry. It is also a beginning, because this moving away from the confining qualities of time and place means that Jesus will be present always and everywhere. It also means that the humanity of Jesus is now within the nature of the wholeness of God. Our God has scarred hands and feet, and knows what it is like to be severely tempted, acclaimed and despised.

In a way, it is at the Ascension that the value of all the risk and suffering involved in the Incarnation becomes apparent. The saving victim takes his rightful place in the glory of heaven, and only that can enable God's Holy Spirit to be poured out in wave upon wave of loving power that stretches to all peoples in all generations.

Amazingly our own parish, our own congregation, is part of this glorious celebration with its far-reaching effects. Each of us, living squashed into a particular time frame lasting merely a lifetime, can be drenched in the power of that Spirit, and caught up in the energising nature of it.

As we celebrate the Ascension we, like the disciples, are expectant with joy at the prospect of the gifts God has in store, and yet still mulling over the breathtaking events of Easter. It is like being in the still centre, in the eye of the storm.

Seventh Sunday of Easter

Thought for the day

God's glory is often revealed in the context of
suffering and failure in the world's eyes.

Reflection on the readings

Acts 1:6-14; Psalm 68:1-10, 32-35
1 Peter 4:12-14; 5:6-11; John 17:1-11

When Jesus prays to be glorified he is looking straight into
the face of a cursed death. At first it shakes us that this imminent time of suffering and apparent failure, of disappointed
rejection and dashed hopes should be what God deems
glory. But of course it speaks of what is at the very heart of
our faith, that our God is a Servant King, and his kingdom is
one of humility and love, rather than success and popularity.
Power and glory are emotive words which often conjure up
images of military strength and empire-building, but God's
power and glory are of a very different kind.

In today's Gospel we see Jesus at prayer, his will and total
direction aligned with that of the Father, ready to be the
human person in whom God's glory will be perfectly shown
through the outpouring of love on the cross. In an extraordinary paradox, the nails of rejection and ultimate insult are
allowed to fasten his body into the classic position of wel-
come and acceptance, arms outstretched. His written accusa-
tion means that he is even given his authentic title to die
under, mocked and despised. And this is glory. This is what
shows the length to which perfect loving goes, for the inno-
cent One to take on all the sins of the world, accept their pain
without complaint or retaliation, and offer them for transforming into freedom and new life at the cost of everything.

In the light of this it begins to make sense that Peter can encourage the early Christians, undergoing severe persecution for their faith, with the thought that to suffer in this way, in Christ's way, is the earth where glory flowers. To undergo suffering beautifully, by the grace of God, is to have the Spirit of God in all his glory resting upon us, and the privilege of witnessing to God's strength and capacity to transform and redeem anything.

We are nearing the end of this season of Easter, as the disciples were nearing the end of their earthly understanding of who Jesus was. Having gone through death and accomplished his work on earth, Jesus' risen life will take him out of the world, in one sense, but only in order to be right in the centre of faithful lives across the world and the centuries. Just as the angels at the tomb had asked the disciples why they were looking for Jesus in the place of death, when he was alive, so now, as Jesus is hidden from their sight and returns to heaven, the angels ask why the disciples are peering up into heaven.

We can all get far too bogged down in the technical details, which don't actually matter that much. What does matter is that Jesus hasn't gone away and left us, but is going to be with us and in us as we make ourselves increasingly available for his loving service.

Pentecost

Thought for the day

With great power the Spirit of God is poured out on the
expectant disciples.

Reflection on the readings

Acts 2:1-21 or Numbers 11:24-30; Psalm 104:24-34, 35b
1 Corinthians 12:3b-13 or Acts 2:1-21
John 20:19-23 or John 7:37-39

Even if the passage from Numbers is not chosen for today, it
is well worth reading as part of the Pentecost reflection
because it expresses such a wonderful delighted longing in
Moses for the Spirit of God to be poured out on every single
person, if only that were possible. The amazing truth is that
Jesus has made it possible. The coming of the Holy Spirit on
God's people at Pentecost is directly the result of the victory
won over sin and death on Good Friday, which became
obvious with the Resurrection on Easter Day.

Since Easter we have been tracing the growing understanding of what all that meant, and where it might lead, rather like
a potential smouldering fire that has suddenly burst into
flames. The disciples had already experienced the risen Christ
appearing among them and filling them with peace and happiness, reassurance and enlightenment. Now, on the day
which celebrated the giving of the ancient law, the new, fulfilled law is seeringly burnt into their hearts; Jesus comes not
so much among them as right within them, in a breathtaking
way which is, in answer to his prayer, allowing them to be
truly at one with him as he is one with the Father. From now
on, the group of followers are collectively the Body of Christ,
breathing the breath of his life, which is the life of God.

That power is instantly noticeable. The Jewish tradition was familiar with spirit-filled ecstatic prophecy, and many recognised that these people were proclaiming the wonderful works of God which had just been revealed to them with a new vitality and heightened perception. But it was even more than that.

Peter sees it as the fulfilment of Joel's prophecy, and quotes those words to the listening and curious crowd with the excitement of one who is aware that this very day they are present at history in the making. It is an extraordinary occasion for the whole nation of Israel, if they will only recognise it. In a sense it is the day when the new Israel is born. For from now on the bright revelation of God's reality, power and mercy, sown in the promise to Abraham and his family and spreading to the chosen nation who were called to be God's light, will be available to the whole world; all believers will be part of that holy nation, filled with the life of the living God.

Pentecost was only the beginning. It was not only to those first disciples that God came intimately and completely in the Holy Spirit. There is plenty of it left for us! Freshly and vigorously in our times, too, God is prepared to make his dwelling with expectant believers of any tradition and any age, culture or personality. It is a terrible myth that the Holy Spirit is only for some, that any are shut off from that inner God-given life. The truth is simple: anyone at all who prays expectantly and longingly for the real, living God to come upon them in power will receive the gift that God longs to give. Let's not get too worked up about the 'how'; that is God's agenda, and we can trust that it will always be in the time and way which is best for each asking person.

What we do need to return to is deep, passionate longing for God, more than anything or anyone else. And God will come and breathe his life into us all, and the effects will show.

Trinity Sunday

Thought for the day

The mystery of God – Creator, Redeemer and
Sanctifier all at once – is beyond our human
understanding, yet closer to us than breathing.

Reflection on the readings

Isaiah 40:12-17, 27-31; Psalm 8
2 Corinthians 13:11-13; Matthew 28:16-20

There are some things which we sense, but which start
slithering out of our grasp as we try to pin them down in
words. Some deep relationships are like this, and some
intense experiences. It is also true of the nature of God.
Whenever we attempt to explain what we mean by the
Trinity we are bound to end up falling short of the truth,
and inadequately picturing what is simply so deep and
vast that it is beyond the power of human understanding.

Isaiah tries to give some idea of the huge scale of God in
relation to familiar countries, resources and natural cycles,
and the psalmist marvels at the God who is maker of stars.
What both Isaiah and the psalmist stress is what that vast-
ness *doesn't* mean. It doesn't mean that the God we fail to
understand is therefore somehow remote and aloof from
us; so transcendent that he can have no grasp of us or our
situation. His very omniscience, or all-knowingness, means
that both the smallest details and the widest sweeps of
space are intimately known by the loving God; he not only
knows about us in our smallness, he cares and is interested
in everything we do and think and dream.

If we take the image of a young baby being suckled, we
can see that here the baby has a wonderful sense of what

being loved, cared for and nurtured is all about. Yet all it can do is gurgle its understanding, and is probably more likely to express that knowledge by falling asleep, trusting and satisfied.

That is rather how it is with us. To understand the nature of God, and what the Trinity really means, is in one sense always beyond our scope as humans. God is never going to be quantifiable in human terms because he far surpasses what it means to be human. But in another sense we are able to understand his nature as we experience relationship with him and feel his love, nurturing and committed care. All our attempts to express that are rather like a baby's gurglings, or a contented and trusting tranquillity which shows in our lives.

The great commission, which Matthew records, sends the disciples out into the whole world to baptise people in the name of the Father, the Son and the Holy Spirit – the one God is all his completeness and community. It is the relationship with this God which transforms his people, rather than an impossible definitive explanation of it. That is expressed in the other part of the great commission: 'I will be with you always, to the end of time.'

Proper 4

Thought for the day

Wise listeners build their lives up on the strong rock
of the word of God.

Reflection on the readings

Deuteronomy 11:18-21, 26-28; Psalm 31:1-5, 19-24
Romans 1:16-17; 3:22b-28 (29-31); Matthew 7:21-29

Those whose homes are built in an area of clay or sand will
be familiar with the extra insurance required. Prolonged
dry spells following heavy rain are notorious for causing
ominous cracks. In such areas underpinning is a common
sight – manufactured rock foundations out of reinforced
concrete. Jesus' example still holds today: lives built on
rock foundations last without ending in ruin.

There was plenty of rock in the landscape of the
psalmists, who would often use the reassuring security
and permanence of it to describe God and, by extension,
God's law – the words of God. Rather as we might stick
revision facts to the bathroom mirror, or leave scribbled
notes about swimming kit by the front door, the hearers of
Deuteronomy are advised to strap reminders of the Law
everywhere, so that it becomes really soaked into their
everyday life. It is all aimed at turning hearers into doers,
at getting that Law turned into a holy people.

Of course, it was no easier for the people of Israel to keep
up their practice of God's Law than it is for us to keep up
our violin or German-speaking practice without a weekly
lesson. We all need the constant nagging nudge which the

strapped-on law boxes were designed to provide. But besides being strapped on to the outside of us, they really need strapping to our hearts. And that is what the Holy Spirit can do for us, setting our hearts on fire with such love for our God that we long to spend ourselves in pleasing him and working for the coming of the kingdom. Yes, it is certainly wise to build on the words of God, but wisdom is itself one of the gifts that grows out of love – love for the One who has freely given us the freedom we could never achieve by ourselves.

Proper 5

Thought for the day

Jesus' life of healing and compassion acts out God's
desire for mercy rather than empty sacrifice.

Reflection on the readings

Hosea 5:15-6:6; Psalm 50:7-15
Romans 4:13-25; Matthew 9:9-13, 18-26

Last week we were looking at the dangers of giving empty
lip-service to Christ, yet not being prepared to put his
teaching into practice in our lives. Today we look at
another danger – of going through the motions of following God, but without our hearts being in it, and without
any real acknowledgement of the sacrificial cost involved.

What was basically wrong in the story of Matthew's
calling? At one level we can accept that the religious leaders
are justified in pointing out to Jesus that he is associating
with those whose lives appear to have deliberately rejected
God's values. Surely these people are a disgrace to the name
of the chosen nation of Israel? How are they a light to the
rest of the world? The speakers know that they themselves
have deliberately chosen to keep the sacred law, and follow
all the teachings to the letter. They know they are doing
their bit to uphold the values of a chosen people set apart
for God. So far, so understandable. If we are honest, how
would we feel if Jesus came and spent more time with the
gang smashing into our church and spray-painting it, than
with us in our specially prepared Bible studies?

The crunch comes with the attitude of the religious leaders
to what Jesus is doing with these 'sinners'. Had they been
genuinely seeking to uphold God's values of mercy and

justice, they would have had an openness which looked curiously at what Jesus was doing and tried to understand it. They would have noticed the gradual change in the 'sinners' and suddenly realised with excitement and delight that, although Jesus was acting unexpectedly, he was actually helping these people to healing and wholeness. They would then have been there rejoicing with Matthew and the others, and nothing could have given Jesus greater joy.

As it is, they disassociate themselves from the healing work of God; they are, in a sense, selling their true birthright for a bowl of broth. Jesus listens to their complaints, and we can imagine his heart aching at their blindness. He gives them a clue as to what he is doing, by talking about sick people and doctors. They must have reacted to that, not with sudden insight and joy but with supercilious self-righteousness which told Jesus they knew better; these people were evil, not sick, and if he was really a religious teacher he would know they should be avoided and rejected for the purity of the nation. Such an attitude was an appalling insult to the God of mercy and compassion, and brought out Jesus' passionate response: 'Go and learn what this text means . . . and start getting your priorities right!' The whole point of Jesus coming was to do this work of loving sinners into a right relationship with the God of their making.

The story is a sobering one. What had begun as well-intentioned ways of lavishing true worship on the living God had become distorted into worship of empty systems and rituals, to the extent that, when faced with the genuine active presence of God, it was not even recognised. We need to come back, constantly, to the heart of worship, to the feet of God, and listen intently to what he is saying, so that our worship expresses our loving service to the loving God.

Proper 6
Sunday between 12 and 18 June inclusive
(if after Trinity Sunday)

Thought for the day
Jesus sends his ambassadors out to proclaim God's kingdom and bring hope and peace of mind to the harassed and lost in every age.

Reflection on the readings
Exodus 19:2-8a; Psalm 100
Romans 5:1-8; Matthew 9:35-10:8 (9-23)

Stand on any railway station at rush hour and you see the harassed and tense faces all around. Perhaps that is an unfair place to pick, but it is noticeable that the stress and conflicting demands and expectations, and the relativism of our society, which places huge pressures on individual choice of action, combine to make 'peace of mind' a yearned-for impossibility for many. Today's readings speak quite a lot about hope, and being at peace with God and oneself.

In the passage from Exodus we find the people of Israel being given the hope of becoming the treasured possession of God, of being a kingdom of priests and a holy nation, if they are prepared, as a whole community, to work with their God rather than against him. We hear their confident response: 'We will do everything the Lord has commanded.' What poignant reading this must have made for those in exile, with the scattered trail of sin and rebellion behind them. What poignant reading it makes for us as we think back to promises confidently made and subsequent failures!

The wonderful thing about Christianity is that it speaks hope, not to a non-existent strong people who can save themselves, but to the reality of a well-intentioned and blundering race who know that saving themselves is not one of the things that humans can do.

In the reading from Matthew we feel Jesus' fondness and longing for the people, whom he describes as harassed and disturbed, agitated and without peace. He urges his disciples to join him in praying earnestly for more workers in the harvest, knowing that God will be dependent on human co-operation and availability to accomplish the healing and gathering in. That is just as true for us today as it was then, and we need to take Jesus' urgency to heart. True religion is being at peace with God, and the absence of that peace is obvious in our society.

Immediately after this, the twelve are sent out, in the role of ambassadors, to proclaim the kingdom of God and accompany the news with signs of healing. All the detailed instructions they are given point to a loving commitment which is total and without ambition, personal gain or personal comforts. That still needs to be our attitude, as the Church, so that our motives are transparent and uncluttered by sub-agendas or empire-building. We are called simply to love people into the kingdom, where they can know the joy and hope of being at peace with God.

Hope is an intriguing word. It is a mixture of desire for something and expectation of getting it. If either of those is missing, it isn't hope, and if either is overbalanced, there is no peace. But when you have both in balance, hope makes you very happy and contented in the present, as well as in the fulfilment. Paul addresses this phenomenon in his letter to the Romans. We are justified by faith, or provided with an 'honorary pass' to God's presence through Jesus' self-giving death, rather than trying hopelessly to earn it. It is this which gives us freely the illusive peace we all crave.

This is not just for the good times but for the grim ones as well. The kind of love that was ready to die for us when we were God's enemies, in effect, is hardly going to let us down now that we have been reconciled to God. We can be assured that our loving God will provide everything we need in the way of support and comfort during the worst sufferings life may throw at us. In fact, it is his love in us that enables us to grow and develop through such times.

Proper 7

Thought for the day

When we are willing to take up our cross with Jesus we
will also know his risen life.

Reflection on the readings

Jeremiah 20:7-13; Psalm 69:7-10 (11-15) 16-18
Romans 6:1b-11; Matthew 10:24-39

There is a fundamental paradox in the Christian faith
which sounds like nonsense and yet turns out to be true
when you try it. Today's readings paste it up large so that
we cannot avoid it, however much we might like to. It is
the claim that through death you gain life. In fact, it goes
even further: unless you take on death you cannot know
life. How on earth can this really be true?

We all know that our strong life-force, or libido, works
constantly for our survival. Our brains use vast quantities
of energy in supporting life systems and keeping us alive.
There are all kinds of emergency strategies that kick in
when anything threatens our survival, and the body is so
good at managing these that it all goes on without us
noticing, most of the time, and while we are occupied in
other ways. Had it not been so, the human race could not
have continued for as long as it has, nor succeeded in a
fraction of its remarkable achievements. How does 'taking
up our cross' and 'losing our life for his sake' fit in with
this?

There is much value today placed on self-confidence
and self-assurance, in an effort to help people become

their true selves without being so vulnerable to abuse or pressure from others. Self-assertiveness is the quality to prize, and any deliberate giving-up of one's rights is viewed with suspicion and often considered weak and wrong. How does this fit in with Jesus' teaching that whoever gains his life will lose it, and whoever loses his life for Christ's sake will gain it?

We cannot get away from the fact that this is a hard teaching to accept. It requires a drastic and complete change of values and direction in life. It can hurt. It is very costly. Jesus wants his potential followers to understand the full implications of commitment. So why would any normal person want to 'lose' their life like this by choice?

Jesus' answer has been experienced and found to be true by many people in each generation. Just as the result of Jesus' total self-giving in death was new, resurrection life, so the result of us giving up our natural self-centredness is a new sense of life in which we find we are more free to be ourselves than if we had slaved over it. It is the answer of a God who loves and cherishes us.

It is like the difference between a tissue-paper flower and an alpine meadow in spring. The kind of fulfilling life we think we are going to gain by accumulating wealth and prestige at other people's expense, over-indulging our tastes, and feverishly totting up as many experiences as possible in case we lose out on anything, turns out to be disappointing and never as satisfying as we had hoped; there is always something else we really must have or try. In comparison, the way of Jesus gives an inner sense of rightness, calm and integrity, which is very richly fulfilling and enables others to become their true selves as well.

Proper 8
Sunday between 26 June and 2 July inclusive

Thought for the day
As Christ's people we are no longer slaves to sin,
but available for righteousness.

Reflection on the readings
Jeremiah 28:5-9; Psalm 89:1-4, 15-18
Romans 6:12-23; Matthew 10:40-42

Some people are unfortunate enough to suffer from vertigo,
and find that when they are perched anywhere high there is
a terrible urge to throw themselves off into that space
beneath them. They have to back away from the edge for
fear of plunging to their death. It is as if the space commands
them and they have to fight against it. Sin is like that. It pulls
us strongly towards our death, and we have a real battle to
fight against that urge to go along with its pressurising command. Even while we know that sin is bound to be damaging to us, to those we love, and to our world, our wills and
emotions can still drag us over the edge into behaviour
which leads to death. As Paul says, it is like being a slave to a
tyrannical master, obeying its commands and feeling
'owned' by it. It can seem impossibly difficult to imagine
how we could ever break free.

Holding on to Christ, through the cross where that grip
of sin has been broken for us, leads us into a completely
different place. Sin will still attempt to pull us over, but the
power of Christ living in us enables us to back away from
the edge as free agents, rather than slaves. It is as if, rather
than being drawn to look down into the strangely enticing
death-fall all the time, we can enjoy the loftiness of the
breathtaking view without fear.

It is interesting that Paul talks of sin earning death, which implies hard, wearying work. That is true: living enslaved to sin drains us of energy and wears us down. In contrast, righteous living is not a heavy duty, but a loving, happy response to a personal free gift.

In today's Gospel we are reminded that anyone responding to one of God's people will actually be responding to their God. This suggests that our behaviour as freed slaves will be obvious to those around us, since we will be behaving differently. Our attitude and outlook will be open and available to good, rather than knotted up with fear and self-absorbed in our own wants and demands. We will be more ready to speak out God's words rather than pandering to what we think people will want to hear, so that we are popular. But it is important to realise that this change is a natural result of responding to God's love, and not an unhealed determined effort in which we remain slaves.

Proper 9

Thought for the day

To all who are weary with carrying heavy burdens in life,
Jesus offers rest for our souls and unthreatening relief.

Reflection on the readings

Zechariah 9:9-12; Psalm 145:8-14
Romans 7:15-25a; Matthew 11:16-19, 25-30

The first of today's readings, from Zechariah, gives us a clear image of peace and humility, as we hear of a king entering in triumph, but on a donkey. It is an image which Jesus made his own, and it speaks of a king totally in touch with the ordinary people and their needs, an unpretentious king who is unimpressed by the worldly idea of wealth and power, and is not in the business of domination and threat, but openness and integrity.

The psalmist pours out a whole list of God's wonderfully supportive and gracious qualities, in the knowledge that this God-king's kingdom is not like the earthly temporary and fickle ones, but everlasting in its goodness.

So when we meet with Jesus in today's Gospel, what we find is completely in keeping with the discernment of those Old Testament writers who had waited on God and trusted him. Jesus' heart goes out to all who are weighed down in their lives, and his welcoming offer is not to do with domination, or strict rules which terrify with their potential for failure. Instead, Jesus shows himself open and unarmed, offering relief and rest for our souls, through becoming joined, or yoked, with his life in the living God.

It is all so simple in contrast with the complexities we struggle to handle when we are not at peace with God. And this very simplicity, while welcomed with joy by anyone ready to hear it, conscious of their failure to achieve it on their own, is also what brings out the childishness in those who petulantly reject God's help, manufacturing one reason after another to justify their rejection. Sadly, it is often those who pride themselves on their learning or mature, independent thinking, who continue to see Jesus' offer of rescue as a threat and an insult to their maturity and success.

With sorrow Jesus sees the religious leaders of his own people behaving like a bunch of quarrelsome children: they complain, but there is no pleasing them! While they are behaving in this childish way, unable to take advantage of what God is doing in their lifetime, it is largely the ordinary, uneducated crowds who are responding with childlike openness and spiritual maturity.

The same is true in every generation, including ours. While we are never meant to leave our brains at the church door, it is also true that sophisticated cynicism or intellectual smugness can blind us to the true value of our great, saving God coming to us meekly on a donkey.

Proper 10
Sunday between 10 and 16 July inclusive

Thought for the day
Seed of God's word, sown in good soil, watered by his rain and warmed by his sunlight, produces a good crop of spiritual fruit.

Reflection on the readings
Isaiah 55:10-13; Psalm 65:(1-8) 9-13
Romans 8:1-11; Matthew 13:1-9, 18-23

We have a wonderful picture of God's faithfulness given to us every year in the round of the seasons, as the bare earth receives the winter weathering before the seed is sown and the growing begins, leading through the warmth of summer to the gathering-in of the harvest in autumn. It is still relatively recently that all this was basic to our everyday lives, and we still get nostalgic about it, even if we have lived all our lives in the centre of a city.

It is not surprising that many biblical images are to do with this annual round and the desperately important blessing of rain. Today's passages from Isaiah and Psalm 65 give us an ancient lesson on the water cycle, beautifully and wonderingly observed. Isaiah uses it to illustrate the way God's word has a habit of being accomplished, working its way down into the human condition and providing all that is necessary for what has been spoken to come about. It may sometimes look unpromising, but, then, so do bare earth furrows unless you have lived through a previous summer. We sometimes need to trust Isaiah's words during our darker, barer seasons of life.

In today's Gospel we are aware that Jesus has been out walking this same earth we inhabit, watching the yearly sowing of seed and hearing the squabbling birds. It speaks to him vividly of the different ways we all respond to the word of God, and, prophet that he is, he tells it out straight as it is. Leaving people to puzzle over his story is an important part of the process of sowing the seed. It gives that seed a good start, wriggling it well down into the hearer's being as curiosity rolls it around before sleep or in conversation in the firelight. What is this seed which takes root and grows fruit in good soil? What was he really telling us? Growing opposition to Jesus' ministry also makes the parable a safer method of teaching. Perhaps it will serve to soften up the ground of defensive hearts in a less threatening way.

The disciples are surprised to hear Jesus using such a learned method of teaching for them and the crowds. Unlike the crowds, they are at least able to ask him to spell it all out clearly for them. Inevitably, they and we are bound to ask ourselves serious questions about where we are, and how we are responding to the word of God. Presumably the ideal is for the Church to be filled with seed growing in good soil, for all that requires is to be open and receptive, nourished and developed in the watering and warming of God's love. And those of us who prepare the ground need to check that we are providing the very best environment for the seed of God's word to grow strong.

Proper 11

Thought for the day

God's justice is always blended with mercy
and loving kindness, so that we have real hope.

Reflection on the readings

Wisdom of Solomon 12:13, 16-19 or Isaiah 44:6-8
Psalm 86:11-17; Romans 8:12-25; Matthew 13:24-30, 36-43

We are usually quick to complain if something is unfair, provided we or our loved ones happen to be on the losing end. Most shoppers will more readily point out short-changing than over-changing. We watch our children's developing sense of fairness with wry sympathy as they experiment with changing the rules in their favour whenever they start to sense things going against them. It takes maturity to accept fairness whether we gain from it or not. Also, the more complex the situation, the less clear it is to see what is actually fair. Our whole lengthy judicial system is built on the recognition of this.

The Old Testament writers, contemplating God's nature and open to his truth, could discern that in the eternal Being of all truth, justice by itself would be insufficient, and was in fact softened with the compassionate quality of mercy. Mercy can only come from one who has the power, right and authority to punish, since it involves waiving one's right, or even the absolute justice of deserved punishment, in the light of loving concern for the wrong-doer. It is this blend of justice and merciful loving kindness which is a hallmark of the nature of our God.

For a race of beings who know all too well their capacity for making stupid mistakes and deliberate wrong choices, this is all very good news which makes us able to have hope. If we are brave enough to look candidly at our lives we can easily see that justice alone would leave us in a pretty poor state. We would all be poked to death by accusing fingers of absolute fairness accumulated over a good few years of blundering and sin. There would be no hope for us at all.

We catch a glimpse of this inevitable condemnation when we think of the way we are often particularly harsh and critical ourselves about other people's failings which are similar to our own, or about faults we feel we have managed to overcome. What causes this is a large helping of self-righteousness, fuelled by a sense of fairness but lacking in mercy. Thankfully, God holds his love for us as paramount in all his dealings with us, as the life and death of Jesus clearly shows.

In the passage from Romans, Paul's whole argument is grounded in the certainty that we are ultimately safe in the hands of our God, and in Jesus' parable of the wheat and darnel we have a tender picture of God's loving forbearance tempering his justice. How can we, who claim to love such a God, do other than follow this example in our own dealings? Revenge of any sort must be out for us, as must a rigidity of fairness which refuses to look at each individual situation through the eyes of compassion. It is not for us to take God's judgement into our own incapable hands, but to recognise with humility that we all stand condemned, were it not for the amazing merciful love of God, which has dropped the charges and set us free.

Proper 12

Thought for the day

Jesus, the teacher, enables the ordinary, unlearned people
to understand God's wisdom – the eternal laws of his
Father's kingdom.

Reflection on the readings

1 Kings 3:5-12; Psalm 119:129-136
Romans 8:26-39; Matthew 13:31-33, 44-52

It is with disarming and endearing humility that Solomon
prays, as he stands at the starting line of his reign, overwhelmed by the impossibility of the task ahead and very
conscious of his lack of experience and the heaviness of
responsibility. It is typically at those times when we are
acutely aware of our dependence on God, that God can act
with power in our lives. The wisdom which Solomon
requests is to do with having a heart which is skilled in listening, so that good can be distinguished from evil. In a world
where every situation has many facets and interrelated
issues, the gift of wise discernment is desperately needed by
all with decision-making authority. And, as God's reply
makes clear, to desire such a gift is entirely in keeping with
his will.

It is a gift which is increasingly recognised and valued by
those in management training, so that look-alike versions
are marketed to reproduce the actions while bypassing the
more costly genuine listening heart.

In Romans, Paul establishes the reality of the situation: we,
like the young Solomon, find ourselves having to admit that
we are very weak in many ways, and do not even know
how to pray adequately. Yet God recognises our groans and

mutterings of prayer as beautiful in intent, and the Spirit in us pleads through that, aligning our prayer to what is in harmony with God's will. God is on our side. That means he is in no way going to condemn or reject us, and there is nothing at all that can ever separate us from his love.

This knowledge, which is heart knowledge, turns lives upside down and remakes them, alters long-held priorities, and opens up all kinds of possibilities for life-spending. We cannot grasp this truth about God's loving personal relationship with us and remain unchanged. In today's Gospel Jesus gives a whole series of images to help us understand what it is like to glimpse the kingdom of God and enter it.

We are told about the excitement and often the surprise of discovering it, upon which everything we presently value seems so insignificant and temporary in comparison that as a matter of urgency we want to give up all that keeps us from owning such a possession. We are told of the way it grows and spreads with astounding effect, so that not only our own lives but the lives of many others are affected for great and lasting good. We are urged to take this teaching seriously to heart, because the consequences of how we lead our lives here are not insignificant or temporary or a matter of personal taste. It is all much bigger than that, and Jesus does not want his hearers, whom he loves, to reach the end of their earthly lives and find they are totally unprepared for the next phase of life and the consequences of living habitually tied to selfish wants.

He hopes for us to cherish both the ancient wisdom of God's guidance through the law and the prophets, and also the new, heady joy of having God's Spirit breathing through our being with the power and forgiveness that makes living good lives an outpouring of thankfulness to a God whose grace alone makes it possible.

Proper 13

Thought for the day

God feeds all who come to him hungry, and we, as the
Church, are expected to share in that work.

Reflection on the readings

Isaiah 55:1-5; Psalm 145:8-9, 14-21
Romans 9:1-5; Matthew 14:13-21

Supermarkets are very good at placing 'useless' but attractive things right next to the checkout, so that all the children,
wheeled past in their trolleys and bored to distraction as the
shopping is loaded, crave what is on display at a time when
pressurised parents are most likely to give in! Our whole
society is skilled at creating inviting displays of things we
could well do without, and which encourage us in all kinds
of wrong directions. Whether it is the lure to unnecessary
spending in an affluent society, to oblivion or happiness
and well-being through drugs or alcohol, or the lure to join
guerrilla rebellions in areas of instability and poverty, what
we are all after is some gratification which is immediate,
and we are prepared to ignore the long-term consequences
in order to achieve this.

In today's passage from Isaiah, the prophet speaks out
God's yearning for something better for his beloved people.
All these short cuts to satisfaction and fulfilment are going
to leave us unfed at the deepest level of our humanity, dis-
satisfied and craving, but too disillusioned to try the only
truly satisfying food for our souls – God himself. Psalm 145
marvels at the qualities of this God and the individualised
provision he gives us all.

Paul, in his letter to the Romans, lets us catch a glimpse of God's heartache for all humanity, as Paul's own national and family ties heighten his sadness for those in this particular group. They could so easily be with him, revelling in the fulfilment of the scriptures in Jesus, and yet have missed out on what should have been their own heritage.

The Gospel for today describes the feeding of five thousand people. It is a clear picture for us of God's delight in feeding all who have come to wait on him and listen to him. These people had deliberately set out into the open country to find Jesus. They sensed that he had things to say which they needed to hear. They sensed that he cared about their welfare and their lasting happiness and peace of mind. Jesus was himself in need of refreshment and comfort when he arrived, in the wake of the tragic death of John the Baptist, but still his compassion reached out to a crowd of people who knew their need of him.

As always, in every situation, Jesus takes whatever is made available to him and uses it for great good which far outstrips our expectations. As always, he involves his followers in the work of preparation and distribution. In this act of bodily feeding Jesus teaches the people in a living, three-dimensional parable, about the real, satisfying feeding for the soul which can be theirs, and which is the Father's delight to provide. In order to receive, we have to know our need enough to go out of our way to seek God and listen to him.

Proper 14

Thought for the day

God is faithful to us through all the storms of life,
yet our faith in God is so very small.

Reflection on the readings

1 Kings 19:9-18; Psalm 85:8-13
Romans 10:5-15; Matthew 14:22-33

In a sense both Elijah and Peter are sinking, and both are given firm-handed rescue by the loving God. In today's passage from 1 Kings, Elijah is exhausted and worn down, and therefore vulnerable to those nagging negatives which whisper the futility and hopelessness and unfairness of it all. It is a place that many of us will recognise well, and there is rich comfort in the way God responds. First, he has provided Elijah with the basic practical needs of sleep and food, and now comes the spiritual feeding – the teaching that will gather up Elijah and show him new direction and new insights. In contrast to all the turbulence in Elijah's mind and heart, God is noticeable by his absence in the violence of wind, earthquake and fire. The presence of God gradually becomes recognisable in the peace, the intimacy of shared tranquillity.

Still Elijah states his case from his place of misery; God's presence is never kept at bay by such honest aching. But Elijah is now ready to cope with being led out, provided with the new direction and clear instructions he needs. God does not attempt to dissuade Elijah from how he feels, but offers him instead the way forward to view it differently, or as less overpowering and crippling. He does the same with us, taking us through at a pace we can cope with, using where we are as a starting point and gently offering a route of hope.

Peter, too, is suddenly overwhelmed by the sense of his vulnerability, as it dawns on him that he is out in the middle of a huge stretch of dark and angry water, buffeted by the violent wind, and with nothing under his feet except fathoms of cold water. It would be hard to imagine a less secure environment! So how had he got into this precarious and vulnerable place? By responding to Jesus' calling. How vividly this matches the experience of many Christians, responding in joy and enthusiasm to the call of Jesus to trust him and come to him, only to be thrown completely at the realisation of where this places them.

It is all very well to say that, like Peter, we need only to fix our gaze and concentration on Jesus for everything to be fine. But the truth we are shown in today's readings is that there will be moments when we are made desperately aware of our vulnerability. When we take that decision to climb out of our neatly constructed lives and follow Jesus, we open ourselves up to an environment where Christ is our only and total security; the truth of our existence is that we are out on deep water without a boat, and it is only at the moment of this realisation that we begin to learn what faith is all about.

Thankfully, Jesus is always there to grasp us firmly, in our lack of faith, and bring us back to where we feel safe. It is a learning process, and we progress at a pace God knows we can manage. If we compare Peter's performance here with the Peter who boldly proclaims the Gospel in spite of being insulted and thrown into prison, we can see dramatic growth in faith. The environment is no less stormy or insecure, but it is matched by the working knowledge that dependence on the faithful God is all the security we need.

Proper 15

Sunday between 14 and 20 August inclusive

Thought for the day

The good news of salvation is not limited
to a particular group or nation
but available for the whole world.

Reflection on the readings

Isaiah 56:1, 6-8; Psalm 67
Romans 11:1-2a, 29-32; Matthew 15:(10-20) 21-28

The idea of God's salvation being for all nations did not emerge as a new concept of the Early Church. It had been there, intrinsic to that first promise to Abraham, and today's reading from Isaiah is representative of what all the prophets proclaim. In fact, the whole reason for Israel being called as a nation of light is so that other nations can see their way to the true and living God. Zechariah's song at the birth of his son, John the Baptist, sets it all out clearly.

Paul, with a passion for spreading the good news to the gentile world, is equally strong in proclaiming hope for his own people of promise. God is never fickle, and if his promise has been made, it will, in good time, be fulfilled. He can even see how God can bring blessing out of their rejection of Jesus, the source of hope. What that does is to place even the chosen people of promise in the position of receiving God's mercy, spelling out to them his amazing forbearing love.

In today's Gospel we are given an example, a foretaste, of those putting their faith in God who are gentiles. Not only the centurion (who was obviously closely involved with the Jewish people, since he had built their synagogue) but also this Canaanite woman (belonging to a country which was the traditional enemy to God's ways) is recommended by Jesus for her remarkable faith, which touches his heart and impresses him. It is seen in sharp contrast to the 'experts' – the Pharisees who are able to see Jesus at work and hear his teaching with all their background of promise behind them, and are still blinded to the truth of fulfilment.

Such tunnel vision not only makes it unlikely that they will relate to anything Jesus says, but also creates terrible obstacles for other people coming to faith, and that is what disturbs Jesus so much. Self-righteousness, self-sufficiency and cynicism are excellent for stubbing out flickering flames of faith. On the other hand, as we see in the tenacity of the Canaanite mother, perseverance, trust and hope, even in the face of opposition and difficulty, is excellent for building up faith in others.

Exactly how much faith we really have in the true God will be shown not by what we say or claim but by the way we respond and act.

Proper 16

Thought for the day

The Church is the Body of Christ, built on strong rock of
faith and energised by the living Breath of God.

Reflection on the readings

Isaiah 51:1-6; Psalm 138
Romans 12:1-8; Matthew 16:13-20

It is part of being human to ask questions. As soon as children can speak they badger their parents with the constant
'Why?' questions, and that is the way we all learn to make
sense of the world we live in. The deep, spiritual questions
are searching for the meaning of identity and the meaning
of life itself, and it is these questions which are at the heart
of all faiths and systems of belief. They surface particularly at times when a people has its sense of identity
shaken, and today's Isaiah passage comes from the time of
exile, when the people of Israel were having to think
through the seriousness of their situation and the meaning
of it all.

Speaking through the prophet to his beloved people,
God reminds them to look back to their roots and take
heart from the great faith of Abraham, their father, which
marked the beginning of their identity as the chosen
nation. This is where they have sprung from, and God's
promise still stands, in spite of all their wayward stub-
bornness, their blindness and sin. As they recognise the
need to get themselves right with God, the door is once
again opened for progress, and that spells hope not just for
them but for the rest of the world.

For us as the Church, standing at the start of a new millennium, there are bound to be questions about our identity and our calling. We cannot look back over all the terrible costly mistakes without regret and sadness, nor at the divisions and lingering anachronisms which still cripple the spread of the liberating Gospel today. But today's readings are full of practical help and real hope for the Church.

In Romans, Paul encourages us to catch hold again of the joy of sacrificial giving, in every area of life, which he says will actually help us cultivate valuable discernment. We are beginning to recapture the truth that costly giving, in financial terms, is not really about usefulness for a Church short of money, but has deep, spiritual value, and is in fact extremely necessary for us. The cheerful giving nature has spin-offs in all kinds of other areas, including the way we see ourselves as the Church – members, or organs, of a living, working body. No empire-building here, no false humility or boasting, but a loving harmony of people with a commonly held life and purpose.

And the Gospel reminds us to look back to our roots for further encouragement. We, too, share the faith ancestry of Abraham, and all the prophets, and Jesus talks of the Church which he will build on the rock of discerned faith in the revealed God, as spoken out by Simon. Symbolically, he is given the name of 'Rock' to mark the importance of this recognition. The Church is to last, through all kinds of attacks and dangers, cosmically safe in the keeping of the eternal love of God, constantly renewed and equipped for its work in every age.

Proper 17

Sunday between 28 August and 3 September inclusive

Thought for the day

As Jesus prepares for the necessary suffering of the cross, he is tempted, through well-meaning friendship, to avoid it.

Reflection on the readings

Jeremiah 15:15-21; Psalm 26:1-8
Romans 12:9-21; Matthew 16:21-28

The harder we hit against God's will for us, the harder that will appears to be. Today's readings prepare us for the serious business of committed following, and we need to listen very carefully if we are not to be thrown by what can seem impossible demands while we are in the wrong place, and yet which suddenly turn into blessing as soon as we approach them differently.

Jeremiah is thoroughly fed-up with his impossible position. He knows God's hand is on him to be a prophet and speak his word to the people, and he feels that he has made a very good job of sacrificing the pleasures of life in order to be obedient. Yet what has he got in return? Only misery and loneliness, rejection and insult. He complains bitterly, full of self-pity (which always comes from self-righteousness) that it simply isn't fair. God is not that sympathetic, suggesting that he gets himself back to the right place and starts speaking some sense instead of all the moaning, so that God can use his mouth once again to proclaim what needs proclaiming. But he does assure Jeremiah, very tenderly, that he is going to stay with him and keep him ultimately safe through everything he will have to suffer.

It is so easy to get into the worldly habit of trading where spiritual matters are concerned; so easy to start totting up the noble sacrifices we have made, and the time or money we spend for God, expecting tangible returns of our own choosing. Even our intercessory prayer can so easily turn into a kind of bullying of God, or bribery, and, of course, as soon as this happens, we have actually swung round with our backs to the Lord we claim to love.

There is another danger, too. Peter has genuine love for Jesus, and his horrified denial of the necessary suffering is so very understandable. Would we not all react in the same way at the prospect of a loved friend having to go through that? Yet Satan has hijacked this human friendship to tempt Jesus as powerfully as he possibly can: 'Avoid the cross and gain the crown without having to go through all that agony of body and spirit. How will you or your dear friends cope?' Jesus' reply shows us how sharply the temptation has stabbed him, and how deeply he must have yearned, in his humanness, for Peter to be right. But he recognises in it Satan's cunning, and shows Peter that he is, in this instance, not a rock of God's strength but a rock for Jesus to trip over, with all the terrible consequences of that for the whole world.

The suffering has to be. There is no other way. Jesus braces himself for the way ahead, in the certainty that it is for great and permanent good, and that is also the message he needs us to hear and understand. Any cross laid on us will be heavy, and it will hurt, but the loving God lays it on us with such tenderness and as gently as he can. Any cross laid on us is not to do with us only, but has far-reaching effects which we will never realise until we reach heaven and see there the value of the painful journey we have lovingly travelled in God's company.

Proper 18

Thought for the day

It is our responsibility to encourage and uphold one
another in living by the standard of real love.

Reflection on the readings

Ezekiel 33:7-11; Psalm 119:33-40
Romans 13:8-14; Matthew 18:15-20

It is never easy to tell someone you think their behaviour is
out of order. It is particularly unpleasant to do this to a loved
one, or to a member of your Christian fellowship. At the
mere thought of it, we are bombarded by fears of judgementalism and hypocrisy, and the possibility that picking someone up on their behaviour runs counter to the Christian
principles of compassion and accepting love. It is a difficult
path to tread, but that is no reason for dismissing it, and for
too long we have been content to do so.

Obviously, we are to love one another with God's love,
and that will guide us to approach anyone with respect and
honour, regardless of what they have done or failed to do.
But we do one another no kindness by turning a blind eye to
behaviour which is clearly contrary to God's way of living,
or excusing and accepting standards of behaviour which are
against his law of love. There are many cases of people who,
having waded through great suffering as a result of their sin,
have heartily wished that someone had been courageous
enough to challenge them about their behaviour at the out-
set. Through Ezekiel we are warned that any of us who opt
out of such challenging, however difficult it might be for us,
are actually held partly responsible for any evil that results.

Today's Gospel has some practical advice for us in this delicate area. Matthew places it in the teaching Jesus gives his followers about the kingdom. He has just been telling the story of great love and compassion about the way a shepherd searches for one lost sheep until he finds it. It is in the context of this total concern for each individual, and God's loving commitment to the idea of rescue, that we are told to take one another discreetly aside and talk over the problem with them. This is no judgemental confrontation, then, but it is a recognition of our concern, the concern of the Church, and, most importantly, God's concern for the well-being of a loved sheep.

This meeting may be enough, especially if it happens early enough, to bring about a change of heart, or a realisation of the dangers, and a change of direction before the situation gets totally out of control. So often, this is the stage we miss out on, with serious and often tragic consequences for all concerned.

We are given a graded list of courses of action, which, in principle, allow as much opportunity as possible for the matter to be treated discreetly and calmly, so as to avoid the damaging public humiliation and self-righteous hysteria which the media revel in and which is so alien to the concept of Christian love. In the event of all approaches being deliberately rejected, there is the need to recognise where the person is. It is both pointless and dangerous to pretend that what is sinful is acceptable and right. Someone who is deliberately placing themselves outside God's care is doing just that. What they then need is our honest acceptance of where they are, and our continued love and prayer.

Proper 19

Thought for the day

Forgiving is a natural result of loving,
so it is not an option for us but a command.

Reflection on the readings

Genesis 50:15-21; Psalm 103:(1-7) 8-13
Romans 14:1-12; Matthew 18:21-35

Today's Genesis reading is one of the tenderest passages in the Old Testament. We feel Joseph's affection for these brothers of his, who even now are too scared to be honest. We sense his wise, gentle discerning of the real fears under their naïve scheming, and can learn so much from the way he reacts to these genuine fears rather than to the behaviour they present. Out of such wise loving pours forgiveness. There is no question of it being refused, and through the whole experience Joseph can help them to see God's redeeming and transforming.

Psalm 103 celebrates the wonder of God's forgiveness, extending naturally from his loving and compassionate nature and his genuine longing for us to be set free from the hold of sin. In today's section from Romans, Paul is dealing with a question the churches were finding difficult. Judgementalism was creeping in as Christians vied with one another in the holiness stakes, assuming that their way was the only right way of going on. Paul suggests that in matters which are not central to the faith there are bound to be differences, and the last thing we should be doing is condemning what another finds helpful. He points out that God is the one to whom we are all answerable in the end, and since Jesus is Lord of both life and death, there is nowhere that he isn't, or that his mercy isn't, so we should stop bothering with what is really not our concern.

In today's Gospel, it's Peter again as spokesman, voicing the thoughts of the disciples about forgiveness, and a fair slice of self-righteousness colouring their thinking. Peter would have been considering himself generous to be suggesting forgiveness that stretches to the seventh offence, but, as ever, Jesus shocks him, and us, with a glimpse of God's ideas about things. Suddenly we are in a whole new dimension, placed in the position of the one on the receiving end of mercy, rather than thinking of ourselves as the noble one dishing it out to those inferior to us.

Rather like Nathan the prophet, when he used a story to show King David the reality of his sin, Jesus tells a story which begins by making us identify with the servant who owes millions of pounds and has had that whole debt cancelled. Peter, who had fallen to his knees when he first met Jesus and said, 'Go away from me, Lord, I am a sinful man!' would realise immediately that he was like the servant in the story, owing so much and yet totally forgiven. If we imagine Jesus looking into our eyes as this part of the story is told, we are similarly shown what God has let us off.

From this place, the concept of forgiveness is very different. How can we dare to treat others without forgiveness in view of what God has done in us? It isn't a question of totting up scores against us any more, but simply a natural effect of loving.

Proper 20

Thought for the day

We have no right to be envious at the generosity and
mercy God shows to others.

Reflection on the readings

Jonah 3:10-4:11; Psalm 145:1-8
Philippians 1:21-30; Matthew 20:1-16

There is a wonderful candour in the way the Bible records
people's relationships with God, warts and all. In today's
reading from Jonah we find the prophet sulking, angry and
resentful that the enemies of his own people should be let
off the total annihilation he considers they deserve. He
almost spits the words out to God, quoting from the psalms
he knows, and finding God's qualities of compassion and
gracious understanding, in present circumstances, exceedingly irritating!

We have all done it, we have all been there. We all know
how righteous indignation makes us boil, and we take it
out on someone whom we know, deep down, we can trust.
God doesn't come rushing out defending himself against
Jonah's attack because he can see where his prophet is
coming from and he loves this angry ball of resentment
just as much as ever. He gives him time, a little comfort,
and a little experience which enables him to see things
from God's perspective. That is quite typical of the way
God treats us, so it's worth looking out for it next time.

The point that Jonah had completely missed, and that we
so often also forget, is that God does not only love and care
for those we think he ought to. He doesn't share our lines

of demarcation, which label some (usually including our-selves) who are 'deserving' and others who are decidedly not. This has always brought anger God's way, and, of course, it happened when Jesus started living it out in prac-tice, much to the disgust of the religious leaders, who thought they knew better how a prophet ought to behave and with whom he should spend his time.

Time and again in his teaching, Jesus tries to help us grasp something of the nature of God's loving, which is so much wider and more far-reaching than we seem to under-stand. Today's parable of the hired workmen is a case in point. The first lot are happy to agree a day's wage, but they cannot cope with the employer being generous to those who started work near the end of the day. Naturally it is not those paid first who complain, but those who see the arrangement as a raw deal for themselves and resent it. If our basis for reckoning in life is simply what we're worth on an hourly rate, then the longest working labourers have a point.

But the owner is looking at it quite differently, and sees the holistic needs of all the men in the market place, just as God sees all people with their needs and is concerned to provide for them all. Whenever we see God's generosity in evidence, however much of a surprise it is in view of our perceived suitability of the recipient, we have no right to question or quibble, but should be rejoicing with the angels at the amazing love of our God.

Proper 21

Sunday between 25 September and 1 October inclusive

Thought for the day

God longs for us to die to sin and live,
but it has to be our choice, too.

Reflection on the readings

Ezekiel 18:1-4, 25-32; Psalm 25:1-9
Philippians 2:1-13; Matthew 21:23-32

However much we may long for our loved ones to go to the doctor, do their homework or take a holiday, we all know from experience that, unless they share our concern, they won't get round to doing what, to us, seems so sensible and good for them. We may nag or drop hints, threaten or cajole, but in the end it is up to them and we can do nothing about that.

It must be rather like that for God, as he sees what would be such lasting good for the children he loves, and yet must watch us all making disastrous choices, never getting round to tackling our habitual sins, wasting opportunities, and taking no notice of all his hints and teaching, his examples and offers of help.

We can sense that longing for our good and grief at our turning away from it, all through the Bible, in both the Old and the New Testaments. Ezekiel is just one example of the way God keeps speaking to his people through the voice of the prophets, to urge them to look seriously at the consequences of wrong choices and the joyful hope of right ones. Time after time he explains that he is not out to shoot them down, or to condemn; no way does God find pleasure in anyone perishing as a result of leading a life of evil and wrong choices. At the same time, being of nature ultimate truth, goodness, love and justice, it is impossible for God to have deep life companionship with evil, deceit, hypocrisy, corruption or impurity.

We are each of us only responsible for the choices we ourselves make. It is very important to understand that God will never hold us to blame for any evil committed by our parents or ancestors, and any guilt we may be carrying as a result of another's abuse of us is guilt that belongs to them, not us. It is God's will that we should be freed of such unjust burdens.

The truth is that God promises to teach us how to make good choices, and through Jesus he is working within us, inspiring both the will to do good and the act of carrying it out. What the religious leaders in today's Gospel needed to see was that talking about it is not enough; a good choice is completed in the action. It is the son who gets round to doing the work who is recommended, rather than the one who airily talks about it but does nothing.

So we are involved in the kind of caring, encouraging relationship with God which really does enable us to tackle those wrong areas in our life. We are never too old, too set in our ways or too busy to take God up on his offer of live-in help.

Proper 22

Thought for the day

God does everything possible for our spiritual growth
and well-being, but still we can choose hostility and
rejection.

Reflection on the readings

Isaiah 5:1-7; Psalm 80:7-15
Philippians 3:4b-14; Matthew 21:33-46

Following on from last week, we hear today how Jesus
responds to the challenge of the religious leaders to name
his authority and qualifications. First he had met their
confrontation with a return question, which directed them
both to the answer and to their unwillingness to accept it.
Now he follows this up with a parable drawn directly
from their own familiar tradition. As soon as they hear the
beginning of it, they are bound to tune in to the passage
from Isaiah, which is also our Old Testament reading for
today. There is a good chance, therefore, that they will
already be looking out for God's loving exasperation with
his people, in whom he has invested so much and whose
fruit is so disappointing that exile and suffering are
inevitable.

However, although the two parables begin in a similar
way, Jesus' story suddenly changes direction. If the religious
leaders are going to hear anything, this is surely the time
their ears should prick up and their hearts be challenged.
Before, God had found bad fruit instead of good, and the tenderly planted vineyard was abandoned to the encroaching
wilderness. In this story the owner does not come in person

but sends his servants, who meet an appalling reception of hostility and rejection. Anyone already familiar with identifying God as the vineyard owner would perceive that his servants must be God's prophets. So when the story goes on to talk about the owner sending his own son, and the vineyard managers choosing to plot his death, Jesus is telling them in as clear a way as he can about his own identity and authority.

Yet what do we find? The smug reply of the Pharisees shows that they are not yet willing to take on board the implications of this parable for themselves, even though Jesus has brought them to the very brink of understanding. Yes, they can see what a terrible thing it would be to treat God like that, but, no, it can't have anything to do with them, for they are bastions of the faith, are they not?

It is a warning for all of us. We cannot assume that just because we were born into a church-going family, have been to church for years, are on the PCC, or live in a so-called Christian country, that we are immune from the responsibility of making a personal choice to follow Christ each day of our lives. As Paul says in Philippians, he has more reason for such assumptions than anyone, but would cheerfully throw the lot away since finding new life, freedom and joy in Jesus Christ.

One of the reasons we reject God is because he will insist on telling us the truth, and we prefer the flattery and indulgence of self-deception. Yet if we can be courageous enough to allow ourselves to hear him, we gain so much.

Proper 23

Sunday between 9 and 15 October inclusive

Thought for the day

We are all invited to God's wedding banquet;
in accepting we must allow the rags of our old life
to be exchanged for the freely given robes of holiness
and right living.

Reflection on the readings

Isaiah 25:1-9; Psalm 23
Philippians 4:1-9; Matthew 22:1-14

There is a lot of rejoicing in today's readings, the kind of rejoicing which is born of relief and victory, such as was experienced when peace was declared after the Second World War. The images used in the passage from Isaiah emphasise protection and safety in the middle of turmoil, as, for instance, 'shelter from the storm' and 'shade from the heat'. The well-loved Psalm 23 echoes this sense of all being well in God's company, even if we are walking through the valley of the shadow of death, and in both these readings the banquet is prepared by God for his loved ones as a feast of celebration in full view of those who mean harm, emphasising their powerlessness and God's complete victory over evil.

In Philippians, Paul is able to talk about rejoicing in the same breath as suffering. He has trusted God as you might trust ice you have tested, and has found with relief and joy that God does not let us down. In that case, all our time spent worrying anxiously about what might happen is rather a waste of time. Paul suggests that instead of filling our heads with such anxious thoughts we would do better to spend our time contemplating the wonderful things which lift our spirits and make us rejoice, simply hearing them in a list: whatever is noble, right, pure, admirable, excellent and praiseworthy.

We so often slip into the habit of worrying and complaining, rather than rejoicing. At those moments of joy and relief after a difficult or dark patch, we may say to ourselves that we'll never grumble or worry again, because we are at present full of thankfulness; but it doesn't take long before we're back into our old habits. Yet what a lot we miss by failing to rejoice, whatever the circumstances. Rejoicing is a result of trusting God to be the shelter in the storm, and really knowing that he will not let us come to ultimate harm, so that we have, ultimately, nothing to fear.

The parable Jesus tells about the wedding feast once again features the rejoicing and celebration with God which happen even in the face of violent opposition and rejection. All of us can count ourselves among the guests who have accepted the invitation once it is thrown open to those walking in any direction and with a good or bad past life. And it is quite a celebration, stretched over all time and space, heaven and earth. We can afford to savour that rejoicing, rather than rushing on immediately to the next section of the story.

Wedding garments would have been provided, free of charge, so there is deliberate insult in the guest who has decided not to wear his, but remain in the filthy rags of his old life. Jesus wants his hearers (and Matthew his readers) to be under no illusion. Accepting the honour of a place at the banquet obliges us to accept also the grace to be renewed and transformed. Living with our former outlook, attitudes and behaviour is not on, and places us alongside those who have chosen to reject the invitation.

Proper 24

Thought for the day

All leaders and rulers are subject to the ultimate
authority and power of God, the living truth.

Reflection on the readings

Isaiah 45:1-7; Psalm 96:1-9 (10-13)
1 Thessalonians 1:1-10; Matthew 22:15-22

One of the difficulties students have is when there are
exaggerated expectations of emotional returns on money
contributed by parents towards their keep and education.
But, of course, they are dealing with different currencies
here, and the confusion is what causes the frustrations and
disappointments. Today we are looking at another such
clash of currency; our duty and responsibility towards
God and to 'Caesar'.

The Pharisees had simply contrived the question in order
to catch Jesus out, picking one of those 'Catch 22' situations
where you can't win. If Jesus said they should give their
taxes to Caesar, it would be an insult to the national pride of
his followers, and if he said they shouldn't, the Roman
authorities would be able to sort him out for them. We can
imagine the quantities of midnight oil spent planning the
scheme.

Jesus sees exactly what they are planning, and deftly
counters the attack by means of stating the truth. He points
out that in fact the two are different currencies. This chal-
lenges his hearers to check their balance and commitment
both to earthly and heavenly citizenship. It completely
avoids the confrontation hoped for, and alienates neither

the people nor the authorities, so the Pharisees, impressed but no doubt furious, can only withdraw and leave Jesus alone.

It conveniently allows us to learn from Jesus about authority and those in charge. Both the Isaiah reading and Psalm 96 are grand and glorious, proclaiming the total and ultimate authority of God over all creation and all peoples, including their rulers, and in Thessalonians there is the same sense of God's authority as the living truth. These are concepts of cosmic proportion, and remind us of the transcendence of the God we worship. Human authority and empires shrink as we contemplate the reality of God's glory and power. Yet the Son of God, breaking into our human system of life, chooses to walk among the ordinary people in the squalor of their need, and enter the holy city on a donkey.

What does this tell us about giving to God what is God's? Certainly it burns into our consciousness that the great almighty God, source of everything we have, including life itself, is not to be 'paid off' with our small change, either in money or time. He is worth nothing less than everything – all that we are, our past, present and future, freely given back in gratitude and love to the one who has given us so much.

Immediately it becomes clear that our commitment to 'Caesar' is a completely different type of giving. However much earthly rulers may like to think of themselves as close to divine, we are in fact all equal in human status before the majesty of God, and our governmental structures are matters of convenience and useful order to be respected and upheld where they express God's will, and challenged wherever they do not.

Proper 25

Thought for the day

We are to love God with our whole being, and love others as much as we love ourselves.

Reflection on the readings

Leviticus 19:1-2,15-18; Psalm 1
1 Thessalonians 2:1-8; Matthew 22:34-46

If any proof were needed that Jesus had come not to condemn but to save, it is here in today's Gospel. Jesus' response to the Sadducees, putting them right in an area of understanding, had the effect of making some of the Pharisees much more open to Jesus, and this time they come not to trick him but examine him, to sound out more of his teaching on the law, in which they considered themselves expert. They ask Jesus what kind of commandment is the greatest, and this would have arisen from the debates they were used to having with the Sadducees about emphasis. From the Gospels and Letters we can see that current debate must have centred on such matters as right observation of the Sabbath, right giving and tithing, and the question of purification and circumcision. Where did Jesus stand?

Typically, Jesus takes them back to the heart of the matter, quoting a specific commandment, the first, which they would have been assuming intellectually, but which in their lives was being crowded out by all the detailed laws and rules. Jesus was willing to stand alongside the Pharisees as soon as there was the faintest hint of openness, and he shows respect for what they have got right: the law's importance. From the fairly obscure book written for the Levite priesthood, and revered by the Pharisees, Jesus draws out the summary of the law: love given to God first and, by extension, to our neighbour, using the measuring stick of self-love to help us understand its meaning. At least the Pharisees have it in their heads, even if not yet in their hearts.

Answering their agenda of detailed differences with this broad sweep of general principle, taken from writings they cherished, opened up the possibility of truth dawning on these over-conscientious law-keepers. As with old paintings, the years of familiar yellowed varnish needed removing so that the original vibrant colours could once again shine. Jesus patiently chips away, flake by flake. He asks them to look again at the Messianic promises, looking deeper than the traditional snap responses towards a curious question-ing which might lead them to look at wider possibilities of fulfilment than they have previously dared.

With Jesus we are always being drawn forwards, deeper into the love and meaning of God, and he will use all our doubts and experiences of life to help us. We need not be afraid to question where God is concerned, for that is how we learn.

All Saints' Day

Thought for the day

Lives that have shone with God's love on earth are filled
with joy as they see their Lord face to face.

Reflection on the readings

Revelation 7:9-17; Psalm 34:1-10
1 John 3:1-3; Matthew 5:1-12

Saints are not a special breed or caste. They do not possess a
certain prescribed blend of skills, and emerge out of particular sets of circumstances. There is really only one thing
which marks out a saint from the rest: they are the ones who
know, without doubt, that they need God, so they do something about it, and go to him, just as they are and open to
receive from him.

Psalm 34 obviously comes from experience when the
psalmist reflects that those who go to the Lord for help will
have every good thing, and the saints would agree. In the
vision of heaven in Revelation we find them utterly filled
with joy and peace as they lose themselves in worship and
praise. Describing heavenly things in earthly language is
naturally difficult, but this passage gets close to touching
the heavenly in us, and draws us into a sense of heaven's
fulfilment, where there is no more pain or hunger and all
tears are wiped away for ever.

Here is the reward promised in the Beatitudes – reward
in the sense that it is the natural outcome of living so know-
ingly dependent on God's goodness, love and guiding. We
are all called to be saints, and become so in direct proportion to the extent we desire God. That is linked with the

way we perceive him. There are so many who reject a god they wrongly assume to be the God of living truth, and if only they were introduced to the real person would have a very different response. There are others who lavish attention and time on false images they think are true, so that desire for the real Person of the true and powerful, living God is treated with suspicion and renounced.

The wonderful thing about our God is that he searches for us, wherever we are, listening for our bleating, lifting us on his shoulders and carrying us safely home. It doesn't matter where we have been, how bedraggled and smelly we are, or how long we have been lost. As we bleat in our brokenness and long for our Shepherd-God to give us all we need, we begin the path to sanctity, and only lose our way again if we start to lose sight of the truth of our dependence on God's grace, and his unwavering provision.

As John writes in today's reading, to be really Christlike is to see things as they really are, with our perception healed. And that takes us back to the saints in heaven, gazing on the Lord they have been drawing close to throughout their lives, and whom they now recognise clearly. That integrity of perception drenches them in the beauty of holiness, and their eternity is filled with worship and praise.

Fourth Sunday before Advent

*Sunday between 30 October and 5 November inclusive**

* For use if the Feast of All Saints was celebrated on
1 November and alternative propers are needed.

Thought for the day

With God's light and truth to guide us, we shall be
brought safely through to the end of time.

Reflection on the readings

Micah 3:5-12; Psalm 43
1 Thessalonians 2:9-13; Matthew 24:1-14

Today marks a change in direction and mood in the
Church's yearly cycle. We embark on our preparation for the
great seasons of Advent and Christmas, when we shall once
again be celebrating the first and anticipating the second
coming of Jesus Christ. We start with a reading from the
prophet Micah, deeply disturbed by the corruption and
injustice around him, and able to discern the inevitable suffering and pain that is bound to result.

Jesus shares this grief for the holy city. He has been voicing
his sorrow and love for Jerusalem, and realises that Micah's
prophecy of the city becoming a pile of rubble is tragically
true, and not that far off. The disciples are stunned by Jesus'
words, and we can imagine them thinking it through in
silence on their way across the Kidron valley, before plucking
up the courage to broach the subject with Jesus again. They
need to know more.

Jesus sees the waves of destructive forces sweeping
through the next forty years and culminating in the sacking of the city of God. It is an inevitable and natural result

of the coming of the Messiah to a chosen people who mainly fail to recognise and choose to reject him. And so it proved to be. The earthquake recorded on Good Friday began a series of tremors in the area which Seneca, writing in AD 58, describes as spreading devastation over Asia, Achaia, Syria and Macedonia. There were famines and plagues in the reign of Claudius in Syria and Rome, and many wars involving the Jewish people. The letters of John, Peter and Paul warn of the rash of false prophets, and Acts records the Church facing opposition and the beginnings of persecution. Jerusalem fell in AD 70, when the Romans tore it apart so that, quite literally, not one stone was left on another.

Hearing today's Gospel is like witnessing an accelerated film of these terrible events over the space of a generation and throughout much of the Roman empire; we are very conscious of the aching sadness of it all – and the inevitability. Yet it was also the sacking of Jerusalem which scattered Christians far and wide, so that the Gospel was spread rapidly over the known world; it was like the birth pangs as the Christ brought in the new life of the Church.

The reading from Thessalonians is a refreshing glimpse of careful witnessing and teaching, with the good of others and their rescue at heart. It links with the lovely words of Psalm 43: 'Send forth your light and your truth; let them guide me; let them bring me to your holy mountain, to the place where you dwell.' We are left with the conviction that through all the terrible, tragic places we may have to walk on our journey, we shall be kept ultimately safe, through faith in Jesus, and we will have with us the light of his guiding and the yardstick of his truth which will enable us to persevere to the end.

Third Sunday before Advent

Sunday between 6 and 12 November inclusive

Thought for the day

We need to keep ourselves awake and prepared so that
the Day of the Lord does not come to us as darkness
rather than light.

Reflection on the readings

Amos 5:18-24 or Wisdom of Solomon 6:12-16
Psalm 70 or Wisdom of Solomon 6:17-20
1 Thessalonians 4:13-18; Matthew 25:1-13

Today we continue to look at the potentially terrifying
future. The prophet Amos proclaims to the people God's
warning. It is all very well for them to think cheerfully
about the Day of Judgement, assuming that the judgement
will be in their favour since they are the chosen nation, but
if the society they live in is filled with corruption and
injustice, they will have a very nasty shock waiting for
them. It will be, he suggests, like when you reach your
home, where you assume you are safe, and casually put
your hand on the wall, only to be bitten by a snake. The
horror is even worse for being unexpected and suppos-
edly undeserved.

Blindness to reality is a theme which surfaces again and
again throughout the Bible. As Jesus said to the Pharisees
after healing the blind man, if they recognised that they
were blind there wouldn't be a problem; it was because
they thought they could see that there was no hope of
healing. The first and most important stage of healing for
all addicts is to recognise their addiction. That opens up
the route to freedom.

Most of us see in ourselves what we want to see, and have blind spots about areas we do not wish to change. The human brain is immensely good at self-deception, packing in layers of psychological wadding to protect us from truths we do not wish to hear. This is why, if someone trespasses anywhere near the truth we are avoiding, we tend to react with what seems like irrational anger and irritability. In fact, it is exceedingly rational, since we are protecting ourselves from discovering that hidden core.

The risks of living without self-knowledge, however, far outweigh the attractions. The less we live a lie, the more integrity we have as people, and that has benefits for the society in which we live, and for our local church community. A whole group of people with self-knowledge can bring about great good and widespread healing.

The unprepared bridesmaids in today's parable alert us to the terrible possibility of being shut out of the kingdom by default. As we consider the tragic, eternal consequences of living in denial of God's law of love and truth, we need to be brave about those areas we may have hidden from ourselves, perhaps for many years, and ask for God to reveal them to us, so that we can have them healed before it is too late.

Second Sunday before Advent

Sunday between 13 and 19 November inclusive

Thought for the day

The Day of the Lord will hold terror for the wicked and unprepared, but rejoicing for those living in God's light.

Reflection on the readings

Zephaniah 1:7, 12-18; Psalm 90:1-8 (9-11), 12
1 Thessalonians 5:1-11; Matthew 25:14-30

People speak sometimes of being petrified by fear; they are so terrified that the fear paralyses their bodies, and they are, momentarily, 'turned to stone'. There is much in the reading from Zephaniah to petrify. The prophet pours out horrifying descriptions of the Day of the Lord, full of wrath and anguish, trouble and ruin. It is like the shock tactics used in documentaries to terrify us out of speeding, and it pronounces unrelieved condemnation, justly deserved. Zephaniah is a particularly gloomy prophet; the times he lived in were grim in terms of both religious and social corruption, and he still remembered better times to compare them with. Total annihilation seemed inevitable.

But we are not to let such warnings petrify us to the point of preventing change and action. It is good that our Old Testament reading is tempered with the positive, though still serious, words of the letter to the Thessalonians. Certainly the Day of Judgement will come 'like a thief in the night', at a time we are not expecting, but that need not make us over-fearful if we are people of daylight. Christ's coming and his saving work has given us access to the necessary protection against evil, and, provided we make use of it, we do not need to live in terror. We are reminded that it is certainly not God's will that any should perish, and what he longs for is that we should all be saved.

Accordingly, we need to spend our energies as the Church more in encouraging one another, and loving sinners to repentance, than coming in heavy with scare-mongering and condemnation. We should not behave as 'daylight dwellers' through terror of eternal punishment, but through a natural thankfulness as the extent of God's love dawns on us, and his ways of love and truth become increasingly attractive to us.

This carries with it not terror but peace and joy, together with the maturity of responsibility. The kingdom of God is not about people terrorised into submission; part of sal- vation is being given the grace to grow up. Today's parable of the talents reminds us of this expectation in our new life. God expects us to make the most of all we have been given, rather than hiding our gifts away, either out of a mock modesty or a fear which insults the loving justice of God. All these gifts we have been provided with can be used and enjoyed, both for the encouragement and building-up of the Church and in the service we are called to give in the world.

Christit the King

Sunday between 20 and 26 November inclusive

Thought for the day

In total humility, at one with the least of his people,
Jesus, the Messiah or Christ, reigns as King,
with full authority and honour for eternity.

Reflection on the readings

Ezekiel 34:11-16, 20-24; Psalm 95:1-7a
Ephesians 1:15-23; Matthew 25:31-46

There is a glorious contrast between the high office, power
and authority given to the Messiah and the tender humility
in which he acts with his people. This high office is not of the
worldly kind, which tends to take promising people away
from the practical caring and isolate them in managerial
offices where they can easily lose the common touch.

The Messiah finds his true identity in searching for the
lost, bringing back the strays, binding up the injured and
strengthening the weak. Ezekiel the prophet proclaims the
humility of this Servant King, whose mercy and loving
kindness soothes aching souls and reassures us all. It is not
that sin is excused or ignored, but that God longs to mend
whatever is broken in us, and to gather us up, even after
our own foolishness has caused our scattering. Psalm 95
echoes the image of us belonging to God and his kingdom
as sheep belong to the shepherd and his pasture.

In the reading from Ephesians, Paul talks of the great
power at work in raising Jesus from the dead, which places
him in the position of eminence, King of earth and heaven,
and which is also the cause of our hope. In becoming one
with Christ through faith in him, we are brought into the

everlasting kingdom where he reigns, and can rejoice that it is so, since it is not earned by works but freely given through grace.

In the Gospel we reach the end of the series of parables in Matthew dealing with the Day of Judgement. We have seen it from the viewpoint of the Church (the bridesmaids), the leaders with responsibilities (the talents), and now those who live and die without knowing the revealed truth. As all these people of other faiths and none are gathered before the throne of God, it is shown to them how, in their human goodness and thoughtful service to others, they have unknowingly been serving the God of love, and therefore belong to his kingdom, whatever name they may have given it before.

Of course, the reverse is also true, and it is not simply doing harm to others which marks out our rejection of God's ways. It is the goodness we fail to do, the needs we do not notice and ignore. Such blindness works in opposition to the law of love and places us outside the kingdom. The separation of sheep from goats is not so much judgement and punishment as sorting out those already shown to belong to the kingdom of God by their life's intent from those who are already shown to belong to the kingdom of darkness.